The Supervision of Ministry Students

Doran C. McCarty

CONTENTS

DEDICATED:

To my wife
Gloria Laffoon McCarty

PREFACE

This complicated world is moving so fast, how can ministry students ever catch hold of the brass ring and get started? How will they keep from getting mangled when they do? Among Baptists, many congregations have a student pastor so that the problem accelerates. The inexperienced students often get "chewed up" in their early attempts at ministry. On the other hand, congregations suffer at their student pastor's inexperienced hands.

The Rural-Urban Missions Department of the Home Mission Board works with many of the congregations which student pastors serve. Several years ago the department decided that a significant way to help the congregations was to help the student pastors. As a result, a group developed a field education program in colleges, seminaries and Bible institutes which they called "in-service guidance." The fruit of this program has been that many congregations have been aided by student pastors who were helped and supported through in-service guidance. Many different forms of in-service guidance programs exist but the central element upon which their effectiveness depends is supervision. This book has been written to provide a philosophy for supervision and help with specific areas.

I have tried to write the book to apply to all areas of ministry. Beyond that, however, the book has been written to help all parties involved in supervision: the director, the supervisor, the congregation and the student.

A few years ago Tjaard Hommes, formerly of Harvard and now at Notre Dame, encouraged me to write about supervision. My colleague, the late Clifford Ingle, prodded me to write a book on supervision. I made several starts but finally finished the manuscript when I was commissioned by the Rural-Urban Missions Department of the Home Mission Board of the Southern Baptist Convention. Larry Bryson was the first person in that department to encourage me. Later J. T. Burdine and James Nelson (department director) commissioned me to do the book. I also appreciate the support of Loyd Corder and Gerald Palmer of the Board.

I wish to thank my own institution, Midwestern Baptist Theological Seminary, for supporting me in this venture. Also, I want to thank several who have helped me sharpen my perspective in supervision by being colleagues with me in the supervision in the Doctor of Ministry program—Ernie White, Olan Runnels, J. L. Wilson and Bill Link. While many other supervisors have contributed, these peer group supervisors in the Kansas City area have met with me regularly.

Several helped me get the manuscript ready: Glenda Hodges, Shirley Mynatt, but especially Sharon Anders who has worked for so long with me on the project.

Chapter I
The Foundation of Supervision

We are under supervision all the time even if we do not recognize it as such. When we stop for a traffic light at an intersection, we are being supervised. This supervision is by a mechanical supervisor although certainly there is human programming behind it, which in turn represents the supervision of society. Society supervises us through laws, traditions, mores and taxes.

Our earliest experiences were related to a most important supervisory team —our parents. Early in our lives they supervised almost completely our eating, playing and sleeping. Our parents are still partially supervising us through psychic tapes which we recorded during our childhood and adolescence and now replay in life situations.

Marriage is a kind of mutual, team supervision. We also have many other supervisors such as coaches, bosses, doctors and lawyers.

Specific Definitions

So supervision takes place all the time. The issue is not whether we are supervised but whether we have the appropriate kind of supervision to achieve our goals. There can be malignant as well as beneficent supervision. Therefore a definition of good supervision is: providing a support system for the enrichment of personhood and to assist in the performance of tasks.

An important ingredient in developing a supervisory support system is the formalizing of relationships and structures so that the supervisor and supervisee will be conscious of the various aspects of the supervisory task. This formalizing will be an agreement between them about how they will organize themselves to achieve their goals.

The goals themselves are also a part of the formalizing of relationships. The formalizing also takes into account the structures within which the supervisor and supervisee work. The structure may mean that the relationship of the supervisor to supervisee is that of a teacher to a student or an employer to an employee. The structures will include forms of reporting, meeting and dealing with the issues.

Studies have discovered ministers lack appropriate support persons. Our families, schools, network of friends, church and institution of employment are all support systems but they do not necessarily help us consciously learn about ourselves and our functioning.

The supervisor is a major person in a supervisory support system. This does not mean that supervisors will never confront supervisees, because confrontation itself is supportive. It shows supervisors feel strongly enough about supervisees to invest themselves in the supervisees' lives.

One supervisor under my direction recognized this when I talked with him about an incident in the group that he was supervising. After considerable discussion, he thanked me for caring enough about him and what he was doing to talk with him.

One part of my definition of supervision is "to assist in the performance of tasks." While this may be the central focus outside of an educational setting, the performance of tasks is also important in the educational setting because the supervisee needs to function in order to learn from that functioning. Supervisees learn from their functioning so that they can initiate the changes within themselves to reach their highest performance. The basic learning approach under supervision is experiential—a supervisee does a task and then reflects upon that task to learn from it.

Other Significant Definitions of Supervision

Reuel Howe has defined supervision as "the process by which the supervisor helps the student find the meanings in the educational encounter that will contribute to his learning and his competence in that and other situations."[1]

Tom Klink offers a lengthy and detailed definition of supervision based on his experience in clinical pastoral education:

> Supervision is a unique and identifiable educational procedure; it requires as supervisor one who is both engaged in the practice of his profession and duly qualified to supervise; it assumes as student a candidate seeking fuller qualification in the practice of his (intended) profession; it requires for its setting an institution within whose activities there are functional roles in which student and supervisor can negotiate a 'contract for learning;' the roles of both supervisor and student must be appropriate to their particular professional identity (in this case the Christian ministry); lastly, supervision requires for its environment a wider community of professional peers associated in a common task.[2]

David Steere, writing in the *Journal of Pastoral Care* about his supervisor training program at Louisville Presbyterian Seminary, defined supervision as: "... an extended conversation at regular intervals in which the student and a qualified supervisor commit themselves to reflect upon the concrete processes of ministry in which the student is engaged in an effort to focus all available resources upon the student's personal development in a specific role of ministry."[3]

Dick Bollinger, director of the Division of Religion and Psychiatry at Menningers Institute says: "Pastoral supervision is an educational process in which a supervisor-pastor and a student-pastor agree to organize a relationship in a given setting of ministry in such a way as to effect changes in the student as a minister as he does the work of ministry."[4]

Since these authors approach supervision from several perspectives, I include their definitions of supervision to help clarify the task of supervision. Each perspective highlights a particular part of supervision.

Analogies of Supervision

I have found it helpful to use several analogies which describe supervision. One analogy is that of mirrors. We hold up mirrors before the students so that they may see how they are perceived by others. As some mirrors are convex and some more concave, so it is that every person offers a different perspective to the student. Students are able to see themselves as they appear to many other people and situations and therefore they can get acquainted with themselves. They may want to make radical or minor changes based upon how they perceive themselves in these mirrors.

They would never have become conscious of their needs to change or who they are as perceived by others if these mirrors had not been held up before them. These mirrors may be the supervisor's own feedback, the feedback from laypeople, the feedback from authority figures, the feedback from inventories and the feedback from peers.

Tjaard Hommes, professor of pastoral theology, Notre Dame University, uses the analogy of mining. He says that we mine experience and bring it up out of the mine to examine it. This analogy presents the picture of a miner working on a lode and bringing samples out of the mine to the assayer's office for him to analyse. In the same way, students bring their experiences to their supervisors, their peers and others for examination. Just as the assayer breaks down the ore into various components, so supervision breaks down experiences into various components of compulsions, motivations, skills, reactions and understanding.

Joe Gross, director of the Department of Pastoral Care, Baylor University Center, Dallas, Texas says:

The analogy that best describes my understanding of pastoral supervision is that of the old two-man railroad push cart. Standing face to face and each pushing on his side of the handle, the energy is transmitted into the gearbox located in the fulcrum and creates the momentum for the cart to go down the tracks. Supervision, it seems to me, is like an experienced push cart operator teaching a new employee how to best push the handle for maximum economy.[5]

The medical function of taking biopsies also serves as an analogy for supervision. The physician takes a small sample of human tissue and examines it to find out about the health of the patient. Then the lab technician determines the health or disease of the biopsy.

The supervisor also examines only a part of the student's work—rather than the whole of the student's work—believing that such "biopsies" will indicate the general state of the student's functioning. The supervisor puts these "biopsies" through several procedures and examines the functioning patterns with several things in mind.

Anton Boisen gave us the analogy of "living human documents." Supervision leads students to learn from living, human documents as well as literary sources. Students are also living, human documents which are read or misread. Supervision offers to read the living, human documents of the students back to them so that students may know about themselves and how others see them.

While analogies help in understanding subjects which are especially difficult, they are also dangerous if pushed too far.

An important question about supervision is this: "Is supervision an art or a science?" Supervision at its best is both. A good supervisor can and will use "scientific" instruments and inventories. There are methods and procedures available to supervisors which are as scientific as any behavioral science. There are scientific, clinical methods of supervising ministry students which are as scientific for their supervisor as they are in any medical practice. Elizabeth Kubler-Ross, a physician who has gained her fame in examining death and dying, says that a serious problem in the medical profession is that it has become a science and has lost its sense of being an art.

Supervision is not just a science; it is also an art which relies upon intuitiveness and feeling as well as scientific procedures. Art is necessary to supervision because we are not dealing with an inanimate object but a human who has that indefinable characteristic often called "spirit."

One person must intuitively experience another person to learn what can not possibly be communicated by scientific methodology. This makes supervision both an art and a science.

Whenever supervisors rely too heavily on one or the other, they are stopping short of making themselves vulnerable in the supervisory process. If they rely on the scientific method, they stop short of touching the full humanness of the student. When supervisors rely only upon the art of supervision, they become vulnerable to their own subjectivism rather than checking out their intuitions against data which can be secured by scientific method.

The Purpose of Supervision

The purpose of supervision in theological education should flow from the purpose and goals of the theological school in which the supervision takes place. While this may appear to be so obvious that it does not need to be addressed further, unfortunately some schools and faculty members and administrators within the schools have not consciously addressed this question.

There are many reasons for the lack of correlation between the goals of the school and supervision. Many field education programs of supervision have risen out of field work programs where administrative people were responsible for the placement of students in religious work positions so that the students could have an income to stay in school. Field education has often arisen out of the context of these field work programs; the faculty never saw the field work programs as having any relationship to learning but only to provide necessary finances for the students. Whenever an institution began to transform field work into field education, the director of the program often did not have the credentials to be a faculty member and therefore supervision was not taken seriously as fulfilling the educational goals of the school.

Another reason, I believe, that field education supervision has had difficulty becoming a partner in fulfilling the purpose of theological schools is that schools in America have long suffered from an inferiority complex in comparison to their European counterparts. The European university system has produced great scholars, great scholarly research and great books. The scholarly presence of the European schools has influenced American theological schools to be centers of scholarship rather than ministry training centers. While this is not true only with regard to the ministry, graduate schools of theology have often seen themselves as academic institutions rather than professional institutions.

Those of us who have been trained in the classical and theological disciplines have our interest in scholarly academia and, therefore, we reward the thinker. James Glasse quotes from a letter which he received: "A seminarian quickly realizes that speakers at convocations are honored if they are scholars. But if they are pastors they are considered simply sources of inspiration and emotional manipulation."[6] The writer points out the results of this attitude: "The third source of guilt comes from the current downgrading of the parish ministry. The value of the parish ministry is seldom a first-hand experience of seminary professors."[7]

The alternative to theological schools being centers of academic, theoretical learning is their being a training center for those who are planning to enter the ministry. Some schools have taken this approach without attempting to achieve in areas of theoretical and critical theological scholarship and have even disdained such scholarship. Theological education in America created the dichotomy of centers of theoretical and critical, theological learning over against training centers in the mechanics of ministry. Since many theological educators have seen field education as being more compatible with the training center approach, many respectable theological schools have been cautious to invest in field education. However, the notion is growing in theological education that the dichotomy between field education and theological education is not an appropriate one and that we should eliminate this dichotomy. James Spicer writes: "My contention here is the obvious. Field experience and the academic structures in theological education should not be held apart at all; rather, precise coordination and interpenetration should be the goal."[8]

The elimination of the dichotomy between theological education and supervised field education needs to come about for two reasons. When supervised field education is at its best, it is a theological discipline in which theology is taught. Field education does not only teach a person to think theologically but to act theologically or in popular language to "do theology." In fact, field education may be more central in the task of teaching than some of the more traditional disciplines. For example, James Glasse points out:

> In traditional theology, each field develops in relationship to a coordinate 'secular' discipline on which it depends for methodology. Thus linguistics becomes the handmaiden of scripture study, historical scholarship supports church history, and philosophy assists systematic theology. We have become so used to these disciplines around the seminary that they have become accepted by many as 'theological disciplines.' Some biblical scholars, parsing verbs, think they are 'doing theology.' They are not. They are doing linguistics. They are ordering the data for theological reflection. This is important work, but is it theology?[9]

A second reason for the need to eliminate the dichotomy between supervised field education and theological education relates to the purpose of theological schools themselves. They have often gone about doing their tasks—knowing that they were the proper tasks—without ever asking themselves the purpose of their tasks and if their work most naturally fulfilled that purpose. Charles Feilding says:

> The commonest view of a theological school is that its primary purpose is to train students for the parish ministry. With a view to improving educational methods, it is necessary to expl ore the assumptions and the ambiguities which underlie such a statement. Perhaps only the most uninformed would make the mistake of supposing that a theological school was a school for the study of theology, though it is worth mentioning. A minister with only theology would be as useless as a physician with nothing but physic. However, both 'physic' and 'theology' have come to describe the entire body of knowledge and skills required for the practice respectively of medicine and ministry, though in the case of theology the position has never been clear and there has been some tendency to identify preparation for the practice of ministry with the academic study of purely theological subjects.[10]

Feilding's statement tends to make those of us in the classical disciplines of theological education uncomfortable because we see our task of teaching our particular discipline and, perhaps more times than we would like to admit, irrespective that "our primary purpose is to train students for the parish ministry." We have worked hard within our discipline and we want to communicate our worthwhile study to our students perhaps, again, irrespective that our "primary purpose is to train students for the parish ministry." One reason why our ego is so clearly tied to this academic interest is that many of us have moved from the ꞓtudent's classroom to the professor's classroom rather than ꞓrom the school to parish to classroom. Charles Prestwood scores theological educators when he says:

> Unlike schools of medicine and law, there are few persons with established reputations as ministers related to the seminaries. In fact few things cause greater anxiety in a seminary than the presence of a successful minister. There is little dynamic relationship between the men in the profession and the men preparing the neophytes for the profession.[11]

Whether Prestwood's criticism is deserved or not, he reminds us that there are incongruities between the theological schools and the churches and that the ministry is discontinuous with the preparation for the ministry. Charles Feilding put it bluntly: "Ministry today is generally discontinuous with the preparation provided for it"[12] and "theological education does not prepare for ministry."[13]

Whatever direction a theological school takes, tension will accompany the decision. Reuel Howe points this out:

> The debate often waxes hot as to whether seminaries should be centers of theological learning or training schools for the ministry. When we accept that they are centers for theological learning, we may feel uneasy about our responsibility for preparing men for the work of the church. When we accept the responsibility to train men for the ministry, we may feel that they are compromising their responsibility to preserve the faith through the discipline of scholarship. When seminaries try to do both, they feel overburdened. Furthermore, they find the correlation of the two emphases to be troublesome and difficult.[14]

Field education at its best pulls together the disciplined scholarship and training for ministry in churches. This is because field education deals with theological, biblical and historical disciplines as well as training persons in the mechanics of ministry.

The difference is that field education begins with experience and goes toward the theological disciplines to which the student is being exposed or has already been exposed.

This is never easily done but it is especially difficult for those of us who have been trained in the traditional methodology of theological theorizing. Jim Bergland observes: "'Theological reflection' is a difficult concept partly because it emerges in situations where life happens holistically and politically, where issues engulf one in multi-dimensional simultaneity, and where we cannot neatly compartmentalize events in order to achieve supervisory simplicity."[15]

Persons in theological schools need to examine the school and discover its purposes. Then they need to ask: Can those purposes be fulfilled only by classical theological disciplines through classroom teaching? Or do those goals demand that students experience functioning in ministry and examining that functioning by applying to it the grids of biblical, theological, historical, psychological, sociological and organization disciplines?

Task Supervision and Learning Supervision

Unfortunately people often identify the word supervision

with pushing to get a specific task done without reference to any significant learning experience. In an educational setting, task supervision must have the additional dimension of being a learning situation. Supervision in the educational institution focuses upon learning from experience so that productivity is an ingredient in the learning experience rather than being the end in itself.

While productivity is not the only goal of supervision in the educational setting, it must be taken seriously. Supervision within the context of an educational institution is to be a learning experience. Students should learn about themselves, their functioning, and their environment and should see the relevant meaning in all of these.

Charles Feilding and James Glasse describe three types of field work. First of all, *field employment* comes about by financial necessity where students seek employment in either church or secular settings.

The second type of field work is *field service* where students seek to fulfill some part of a societal or ecclesiastical need. Many people believe that this is the viable way for students to test reality and for supervisors to test the depth of students' commitment, but field service may or may not be a learning situation.

The third kind of field work is *field education.* Feilding and Glasse argue that:

> . . . neither field employment nor field service nor a combination of them is necessarily field education. For field education there must be a 'field' where some educational agency can plan and control the educational continuum. This is far from easy to achieve, but nothing short of this can be taken seriously as professional education. Wherever we have listened to reports on student pastorates we have heard of the pressure on the student to make the parish grow. What is lacking is a plan to help the student grow.[16]

It is not enough for students to have places of church employment or humanitarian service. Placements must provide learning experiences or educational institutions do not have an adequate reason to be involved. Students may have church employment without the means of transforming that field placement into worthwhile learning experiences because students may very well practice their mistakes rather than learn from their mistakes. Students may even get ground up in their ministry settings or become emotional cripples for life through their unfortunate ministry experiences.

An educational institution is not a placement bureau, a job broker or a provider of cheap labor for ecclesiastical institutions.

The main function of an educational institution is not apostolic, missionary or evangelistic, but educational. Therefore the field experiences of the students with which the educational institution is involved should be educational experiences.

Achieving Change

The general task of supervised field education is to bring about changes within students while they are in the process of becoming ministers or more effective ministers. The basic change which supervision wishes to bring about is in the inner character and outer behavior of students. These two related areas have a positive influence on one another. Ultimately supervision wants to bring about the integration of the two so that they have a single focus.

Allen Wheelis, a San Francisco psychoanalyst, writes: "Personality change follows change in behavior. Since we are what we do, if we want to change what we are we must begin by changing what we do, must undertake a new mode of action."[17] Wheelis calls into question the common rubric that if we think the right thoughts, we will behave accordingly. While our concepts may influence our behavior, Wheelis points out that much of our change comes about by acting out behavior which makes it possible for us to integrate that behavior into our character.

Another change may come by reinforcing the status quo. Supervisors may find that students have adequate competencies, theoretical knowledge and approaches to ministry, but the students may not accept these strengths nor have an appropriate comfort level while functioning as ministers.

In this situation, supervisors need to help students accept their competence level and be comfortable in performing their ministries. Students also need to understand the significance of what they are doing, or they will not be properly motivated.

Significant change happens to us as a result of our reflection upon experiences. But other things influence us toward change. Whenever we pass through crises such as marriage, divorce, serious illness or death, we are likely to face situations which are catalytic for changing us. Whenever these events come, they are very likely to open the student so that the supervisor can help guide him to healthy behavior.

We have significant persons in our lives as well as significant life experiences. These significant persons can be catalytic for change within us either by the feedback which they give to us or by our identification with those "significant others." The significant others of students may be their family members, professors, pastors or friends. Supervisors will find that they can use this feedback or identification process to help the student make important and needed changes. Supervisors can guide the students toward examining that feedback and how it is applicable as well as pointing out students' need for identification and the helpful or destructive force of such identification.

These ways of changing reflect Allen Wheelis' observations about change coming out of behavior, but not all change has to happen that way; ideas also change people. Noble ideas can transform people into saints and malignant ideas can create monsters. The grand and noble ideas which students get in the classrooms are powerful weapons for the supervisor to use in bringing about needed changes within the student. The scriptures may be the most powerful force which a supervisor finds already available to help in bringing about change within supervisees.

Developing a Professional

A significant task of supervision is to bring about professionalism within a student. The word "professionalism" is not always the most welcomed word within the ministry since churchmen often construe it to mean shallow and perfunctory "playing church" rather than meaningful, spiritual service. I find this an unfortunate connotation since the word is used in many vocations to describe the high standards of committed persons carrying out their role in the best manner.

When I use the word professionalism I do so in three contexts. First, professionalism is doing tasks of a vocation in a manner which has proved to be the most adequate and advantageous for the disciplines necessary within a vocation.

Professionalism cannot be measured by accepting at face value that the educated are professional and the uneducated are unprofessional. Some persons who are uneducated have developed a proficiency and a professionalism in their vocation. Professionalism does not mean that a person will function perfectly but the professionals know what their abilities are and usually recognize the areas in which those abilities can be utilized profitably. Professionals will also realize their limitations and invite other professionals to assist in a particular task. Even professionals will misdiagnose a situation at times because they are not omniscient and there is no scientific way available to diagnose every situation. Many situations, especially in social context, are beyond satisfactory diagnoses. There are situations where the professionalsim of a person does not appear to be adequate simply because the resources are not available to exercise full professionalism. The professional may not have all of the funds available to solve social problems; he or she may not be able to change attitudes overnight within society which would demonstrate the professional answers which the professional knows. Ministers may not be able to exercise their professionalism by referring some people to specialists in other professions because of a lack of financial resources or the unavailability of those specialists. A problem which so often plagues ministers is that they must "make do" rather than refer to a specialist. In these situations, ministers sometimes have to use the resources they have because they are unable to acquire the expertise of other professionals.

A second thing I mean when I speak about professionalism is that there are times when ministers do not feel the charisma to undertake tasks which have to be done but the professionals will go ahead and do the job anyway. Ministers may be "down" at times, as far as their own mental attitude is concerned, and may not feel like preaching. This does not mean they do not have something important to say, but it may mean they are catching the flu, suffering from rheumatism or are in the depressive stage in their manic-depressive personalities. Professionals are not limited by the emotions of the moment but recognize that a call goes beyond that particular moment.

During World War II, a minister was told about the telegram that had just informed a parishioner that he had lost his soldier-son in combat. The pastor refused to make a pastoral call on the bereaved family and tried to justify it by saying that he did not know what he could say to them in such a tragedy that they did not already know. The pastor was guilty of unprofessionalism. A professional would have gone and shared of himself whether or not he had the magic formula of words.

The third thing which I mean by professionalism is that a professional has reached a level of competence and wants to share that competence with others. The professional offers a disciplined way to help others reach professionalism. This may be the highest level of professionalism.

Supervisors are in the business of transforming neophyte students into professional ministers. They are not to give their stamp of approval to dilettantes in ministry.

Competence in Ministry

James Glasse says that competence in ministry is the "... operational understanding of...ministry...."[18] Glasse introduces two areas in this definition of competence. They are cognitive and functional areas. Ministers must be able to function in an effective manner to bring about the goals which they have in mind. They also must know the bases of those goals and the reasons for taking action "A" rather than action "B" to achieve their goals.

Ministers may perform functions without having appropriate feelings about what they are doing, but I doubt whether they are fully professional until they identify the appropriate feelings toward effective functions of ministry. Being in touch with the effective part of their lives is as much a part of ministers' professionalism as the football team taking calisthenics before a game or a baseball pitcher warming up before a game; these are all a part of their professional discipline. The football team might play a game without injury if they do not take calisthenics and a baseball pitcher might win a game without warming up but over the long run, not following their discipline would be destructive. Unless ministers are able to follow their full professional discipline, including an appropriate affective part of their personhood, in the long run they will lose their effectiveness.

The definition of competence in ministry is a necessary beginning, but the frightful problem is the *measurement* of competence. Some goals, such as doubling the attendance or budget, may be easily measured but the value of the worship service is not solely in the attendance but in how the worship service influences worshippers. The qualitative dimension becomes difficult if not impossible to measure.

Many areas of the ministry are not related to physical bodies, buildings or organizations but are related to the souls and spirits of persons. Part of the conversation between Nicodemus and Jesus dealt with the problem of the non-objectifiable spiritual realm. Jesus pointed out: "the wind blows where it will and you heard the sound of it, but you do not know whence it comes or whither it goes; so it is with every one who is born of the Spirit."[19] Nicodemus depended on a religion that was fully objectifiable and he was scandalized at the non-objectifiable element in the "spiritual" religion of Jesus.

Because of the element that is non-objectifiable which is uniquely a part of the human spirit, the development of the methods to measure competence in these areas is tricky business and at its best has limitations.

Often the test of competence is how well one human spirit is the bearer of the divine spirit to another human spirit. After having warned about the impossibility of satisfactorily testing our competence in ministry, I want to say that we must make every attempt to develop ways to measure whether or not we are competent ministers. Schools have developed questionnaires for students to try to do this. The Academy of Parish Clergy has been particularly interested in helping ministers at this point.[20] They have completed a major study project about competence in ministry.[21]

The Association of Theological Schools sponsored a three-year research study called "Readiness for Ministry." This project attempts to identify areas of competence for ministers which the Christian faith in our present world demands of the ministry.[22]

Integration of Theoretical and Experiential

Tjaard Hommes writes: "...Supervision as Theologial Method implies ... the supervisor is a type of theologian."[23] Supervision, as a learning activity, is a theological task whereby students examine their ministry experiences for theological meaning and plan future ministry conscious of theological guidelines. Supervision as a theological task helps to overcome the problems Charles Feilding refers to when he says that: "Ministry today is generally discontinuous with the preparation provided for it."[24] Good supervision cuts down the hiatus between the classroom and the activity of the ministry field because it has a two-way flow. While students under supervision take theological ideas out to their supervised ministry settings, they also bring back to the classroom their ministry experiences to examine for their theological content.

Theological integration in supervision is not accidental because students will have to deal with ministry experiences outside of the classroom setting every day of their lives. It is important for them to begin to see the theological implications of what happens right around them, to see the theological meaning in their experiences and to become conscious of using theology as they minister.

While this subject will be addressed several times throughout this book, it is important that we not think of theological discipline in one arena and supervision in a second arena. I like to think of the two disciplines as though they are two spotlights on the stage which move together in the experience of a student until the two spotlights finally merge into one circle of light.

Personal and Professional Identity

Supervision is to help the student achieve personal integration. Allen Wheelis says: "We are what we do ... Identity is the integration of behavior."[25] Students need to develop the identity of who they are as persons integrating all of the functions of their private and professional lives. They need to have feelings of adequacy and independence when they are in strange places and in circumstances where the usual functioning of their roles as ministers and authority figures are not recognized.

William C. Myers outlines the three issues of personal identity for seminarians. He says, first: "Each seminarian needs to identify and accept his own positive and negative attributes." Second: "The seminarian needs to develop inner processes of self-discipline to replace reliance upon external control." Third: "The seminarian needs recognition and acceptance of his desire for the support and concern of other people."[26] The issue of personal identity is especially an important one for theological students since many of them are struggling from adolescence toward adulthood. They still have many of the feelings of adolescence while being forced to take upon themselves adult responsibilities. Many people, such as their parents, are still relating to them as adolescents even though they are expecting adult behavior and decision-making.

Alongside this personal identity problem of moving from adolescence to adulthood, students are taking on the role of the minister. This adds the problem of integrating a professional identity with a personal identity. Students can expect to experience three particular stances and they must be conscious of where they are with regard to these stances.

The first stance they are likely to experience is that of being uncomfortable with the ministry role and uncertain about what the ministry role means. They are not certain whether they are acting as a person or playing a role as a minister.

A second stance is that of losing their personhood in the ministry role. Trying to overcome their uncomfortableness, they may so identify with the ministry role that they react to situations totally as a minister, sublimating their feelings and personhood.

A third stance is where ministers are able to keep their own personhood and personal identity but are able to use the ministry role in situations where it is appropriate for them to function as ministers.

In his book, *Competent Ministry,* Mark Rouch speaks of the professional identity process as the socialization of the minister. He seems to mean learning the give and take of functioning and the compromises which have to be made to meet the demands of the reality of the world in which the minister lives. This cannot be taught in conceptual form but can only come about in ministers at the feeling level where they develop "instincts" for reacting appropriately and effectively consistent with the Christian faith.

Spiritual Formation

Spiritual formation is the development of the interior life through specific religious exercises such as prayer, meditation, contemplation and devotional reading. Priestly formation has been an important ingredient in the training for the Roman Catholic priesthood but in recent years the interest in spiritual formation has gone beyond Roman Catholic training. The renewal of interest in spiritual formation during the past few years gave impetus to the Association of Theological Schools to make a study (funded by the Lilly Foundation) of the role of spiritual development in theological education.[27]

The proper spiritual formation of students is a goal of supervision. If John Gleason is correct, spiritual formation is developmental and relates to every age from infancy through adulthood. Gleason says:

> Even as Erikson built on Freud, so I am placing a religious overlay upon Erikson's eight ages. I am hypothesizing that religiously there comes a developmental epigenetic fullness of time wherein a particular theological lesson is learned at the level of the unconscious, at the feeling level; that particular theological doctrines are in focus at particular stages of human development; that the way the lesson is learned or distorted profoundly affects future religious lessons and development . . . .[28]

Supervisors will want to help their students examine where their experience is in light of the stage of spiritual formation expected for their maturity level. The supervisors may have to help the students untangle previous religious experiences so they can understand why they are dealing with religious experiences at the present time in the manner in which they are.

It is important for students to shore up the interior aspects of their lives. They will be using many administrative procedures, counseling techniques and literary criticism just as their counterparts in secular disciplines do. This makes it important for them to learn that their own spirituality is a distinctive facet of their personal and professional identity, so that they are not tempted to rely only on secular techniques baptized into religious service.

Discipline

I would like to emphasize that supervision helps ministry students develop appropriate discipline for their ministry including the discipline of personal activities, moral life, education, scheduling, planning, relationships, work, finances and devotional experiences. Discipline in ministry education has become largely a lost art among Protestants. The libertarian view and the modeling after European secular universities has caused modern Protestant theological institutions to withdraw from being responsible for developing disciplines among the ministry students in any area except that of the conceptual, educative procedures. This libertarian point of view may be consistent with the spirit of Jeffersonian democracy but it is questionable whether it is consistent with the history of the Christian church or the needs of the Christian ministry.

There is not one purpose of supervision but several purposes. All of these purposes are attempts to integrate theological education fully with the life and work in which ministry students will engage. When supervision is properly and adequately done and these purposes are met, students will think critically and creatively in classroom and seek the kinds of continuing education experiences which will sharpen their facilities to think critically and creatively. The underlying purpose behind all supervision is to focus the cognitive classroom experiences upon the reality of the world and then to reflect back into the cognitive situation what students have learned from the experiences of reality and reflection upon those experiences.

The Theory of Supervision

Supervision, as any other discipline, stands on a proper theoretical base. If there is a faulty theoretical base the proper practice of supervision will only be accidental. The idealogical base for supervision in the theological context is two-fold: educational and theological. First, I will examine the place of supervision as it relates to the educational theory.

Change Occurs

The first assumption in an educational institution which has as one of its purposes to bring about change within people is that change really happens within people. Tasks may be performed better under supervision but in an educational setting, the purpose of supervision is to learn from those tasks and therefore to bring about changes within supervisees.

There is a law in physics which says that an object cannot pass from one point of space to another point of space without going through the spaces in between.[29] The same is true in the lives of people; they cannot move from position A to position Z without passing through the positions in between. Supervision helps students move through those stages appropriately while giving them opportunity to move to their goals more speedily and easily than they could do outside of supervision.

Learning from Life

The second assumption in supervision is that we can learn from life as well as from books. Supervisors do not despise theoretical knowledge from books (after all this is a book and this section in on the theory of supervision); however, what is found in books is true only because it is the generalization, observation, summarization and distillation of the experiences of life in a verbalized form.

In supervision, learning is by experience as well as didactics. Anton Boisen spoke about "living, human documents" which can be examined for the purposes of learning. Supervision is a process of examining living, human documents in order to learn from them. Supervision is a kind of experiential learning which has been called field-based learning and contextual learning.

The Human Being As a Social Animal

Supervision works under the assumption that the human being is a social animal. As social animals, we do not learn isolated within ourselves but we learn within the context of other people. Supervision provides the social context in which the learning can take place in a realistic way. The supervisor is a social being and as such supplies a part of that social context for the supervisee.

Transfer of Learning

Another assumption we make in the supervisory process is that there can be a transfer of learning from the supervisory setting to the situation which supervisees will face when they are beyond formal supervision. The context of supervision may be somewhat artificial inasmuch as the institution or tasks will not be the final tasks which supervisees will finally be involved with in their vocations. However, we assume that the learning which takes place in a quasi-artificial setting will relate to the setting where supervisees will ultimately serve. Self-examination, getting in touch with one's own self, finding out how one reacts to authority, strain or various groups of people in the supervisory process will transfer to other life situations.

Recently I read in a book where the author referred to Victor Hoag's *Ladder of Learning.* Hoag's chart lists the percentage of learning of the average person related to a variety of activities.[30]

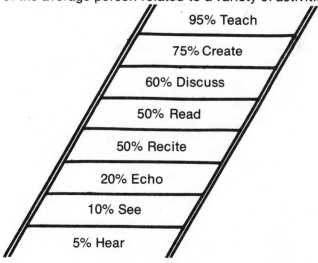

95% Teach

75% Create

60% Discuss

50% Read

50% Recite

20% Echo

10% See

5% Hear

According to the ladder, the more a person initiates activity, the more likely it is that the person will learn. This coincides with the theory of supervision that we learn by doing and examining what it is that we have done.

Non-egalitarian Supervision

There has been resistance to supervision on egalitarian grounds by persons who believe that all people are equal and that no one should be over anyone else. Perhaps this is the way the world should be but it is not the way the world is. As long as children are brought into the world as infants, there is some question whether that is the way the world really should be. An egalitarianism which might function in a Camelot does not terminate supervision because even in a pure democracy each would be supervised by the whole group. We cannot escape supervision even if we resist a one-to-one hierarchical kind of supervisory relationship.

Some people are "over" other people not only because of their title but also because they are more productive, intelligent and confident. The fact is that we need the supervision of these particularly able people if we are going to become more productive and fulfill our own promise. What we need then is not to do away with supervision on egalitarian grounds but to develop a proper supervisory process or discipline so that the supervision will be just, fair and productive.

Three Approaches to Education

There are three approaches to the educative process: cognitive, training and affective. These have been identified in different ways by various writers. Barton Lloyd spoke of "modes of learning:"

> In order to see the goal of personal development of the minister in proper perspective, full preparation for the ordained ministry involves at least three modes of learning and development: (a) *intellectual development* —a man's academic learning, the development of his conceptual and theoretical knowledge; (b) *training* in specific aspects of a clergyman's professional work —*the development of professional skills* and competence; (c) *the development of the man himself as a person* —his personal capacities, attitudes, values.[31]

Charles Feilding speaks of four goals for theological education: Knowledge, professional competence, humanity and Christian formation.[32]

Cognitive Approach

The cognitive approach to the educative process describes the communication of theoretical and conceptual material to the learner. It is the communication of highly abstract images. The cognitive approach is most easily seen in the traditional classroom methodology of institutions of higher learning. The primary tools of this approach are the lecture and the textbook.

Cognitive learning is an appropriate approach to learning and it has been the pivotal point from which we have moved in to other approaches in the educative process. This means that supervision has a high stake in the cognitive approach since it will not be able to function appropriately unless there is strong cognitive input. The major task in supervision will not be to provide cognitive input of theoretical and conceptual knowledge, but neither will supervision be aloof from this task and certainly it will not be hostile to it.

There will be cognitive input in supervision when the supervisors see areas of need within the students and direct them to storehouses of conceptual input. In the main, supervisors will call the students' attention to the cognitive input which they already have and help them relate that cognitive input to the tasks which confront them. The role of supervision is to bring the ideal of the theoretical and conceptual into play with the reality of experience. To put it another way, the task of supervision is to bring the conceptual into focus upon the supervisees' tasks.

Training Approach

Training as an approach to the educative process is the teaching of the mechanics of how to do a specific, functional task. This method of learning is related to concrete functions in doing a task rather than abstractions. Many trades such as plumbers, bricklayers and electricians have long periods of training before the certification. There is an element of training in developing ministers inasmuch as they must perform specific tasks such as baptism, communion, funerals and weddings. The performance of these tasks no more come naturally to the minister than wiring comes naturally to the electrician.

Affective Approach

The affective educative process has to do with the personhood of the supervisee. Affective education is not the storage of factual material, conceptual ideas or the theoretical. Such data is more related to the cognitive approach than to the affective. However, it is true that both the cognitive and the affective approach manipulate highly symbolic images in the respective approaches. The affective approach does not attempt to get a person to function bodily in a more efficient and graceful manner although this might be an outcome of enhancing the personhood of a supervisee.

The affective educative approach is what Feilding called "humanizing." It is dealing with an individual as a human person —helping that person examine how he or she functions, why they want to function that way, and how they fulfill that functioning, how their personhood changes the situation into which they insert themselves and how they feel about who they are, what they do and their station in life. The affective approach deals with what things mean to the person and not just the thing itself. For example, the person may be compulsive about acquiring cognitive information even though he does not wish to use it profitably in a vocation. The affective approach will seek to help people find out about the unusual meaning this has for them. The affective approach also helps the person determine how this affects his function as a human being in the various relationships of life. The affective approach stresses the feeling and the emotive aspect of human living.

Supervision is involved in all three approaches of learning in varying degrees. Supervision will be least involved in the cognitive approach since that will be the main input which students get in their classes. Supervision will be more involved in the training aspect of the student's career. In other places, including classroom, students will learn functions of ministry but supervisors will help the neophyte students learn how to do many ministry tasks both through instruction and modeling. It is at the level of the affective approach that supervision has its most important dimension in learning. It is my observation that few ministers are dismissed from their place of service because they do not have enough conceptual knowledge nor are they dismissed because they are unable to perform the professional tasks of ministry. They are more likely to be dismissed because of problems in the affective area of their lives such as being inadequate in their relationships with people. The supervisor has a keen opportunity to help students in the affective domain because they can see how students function in the context of the pressures of real ministry.

Theological Principles for the Supervisory Task[33]

Supervision, as any other discipline, stands upon a theoretical base. Supervision which happens within the context of the Christian ministry should have a theological base which forms part of the consciousness of the supervisor and is at the last a part of the growing consciousness of the supervisee.

My use of the word "principles" in the title causes me concern. By principles I do not mean for theological principles to be confused with the important task of theologizing. When I speak of theological principles, I mean the theological bases, or better, the theological touchstones as we do supervision.

The Theological Principle of "Ministering"

The word "minister" means "to serve." Others look upon the minister as a person who is in the service of God through service to other persons. The Gospel writers reflect that Jesus' life was in the context of ministry to others: "For even the Son of Man came not be ministered unto, but to minister . . . ."[34] The Christian minister must exercise care so that he/she always performs his/her task with the Christian motivation of ministering rather than being motivated by a lesser motivation.

Supervision helps the student to examine his/her ministry in order to determine the nature of the motivation. The supervisor will help the student keep honest with himself/herself so that he/she does not play games resulting in self-justification by the manipulation of words. The student will have criteria for ministering to others when he/she begins in supervision or he/she will need to develop and articulate such criteria. The supervisor will hold him/her accountable to that criteria with regard to his/her own ministry.

Caring is at the heart of ministering to others. It is important for the minister (student) to have a "pure heart" of caring along with the skills of the ministry profession. The supervisor assists the student's examination of his/her ministry so that he/she may be aware at any point where it appears that the student is only carrying out the functions of an office and giving them the label of Christian ministry.

Supervision offers students many advantages and insights. However, the central task in the supervising process is to keep the student doing and examining real ministry and seeing how the ministry fits the ministering person.

The Theological Principle of "The Value of Persons"

The historic Judaeo-Christian tradition has placed high value upon persons as the acme of God's creation and the bearers of God's own image. A person who tries to justify any action or situation as Christian ministry must take into account the great reverence for persons in Christian scripture and tradition. The Christian doctrine of the image of God (even in human sinfulness) necessitates taking seriously the high value of human personhood. This high estimate of the human person is not because humans are more complex than other creatures in the animal world but because of their relationship to God and subsequently to other persons. A person is not just a creature but a spiritual creature.

Supervision should elevate the dignity of the student because he/she is made in the image of God. The belief in the value of persons means that the supervisor does not take his/her job lightly. The supervisor works appropriately with humility, awe and respect for the student because of the student's supreme value as a person. It is inappropriate for the supervisor to reduce the student to a "supervisory guinea pig." There will be times when the supervisor will confront the student but this should always be done within a context where the student understands that the process will enhance his/her dignity.

The supervisor must keep the student aware of the value of persons as he/she ministers to others. The student needs to render genuine service to those to whom he/she has been assigned for ministry purposes. The student should enhance their dignity and not manipulate them just to "get a verbatim."

The Theological Principle of "Creation"

God created our world and said, "It is good" but that does not imply that God finished the world as a static universe; rather, it is a dynamic universe with life, change and growth still ahead. The Genesis theologian implies that the human race is a partner with God in the continuing process when referring to the command to name the species. While we are not creators in the same sense as God, we are made in the image of God and share the characteristic of creativity. Our lives began unshaped and we were given the responsibility and stewardship for developing their potentiality into actuality. Self-realization may not stand alone as an ethical theory but it is a Christian ethic when the theologian grounds it in the Christian doctrine of creation.

Just as God created a dynamic world, God created persons to be growing, actualizing beings. Supervision holds personal growth and self-realization as significant goals. An important function of a supervisor is to provide the student help in self-understanding in order to unlock future growth.

The student will need to understand himself/herself, which includes his/her past, in order to grow and create. However, the student should avoid becoming obsessed with self-understanding oriented toward the past so that he/she fails to apply self-awareness to future growth. The supervisor becomes a partner with God and the student to help finish the creation begun at conception. The student's task is not just to work but to grow through work. The student is to affirm the creative process by bringing possibilities to reality. The supervisor provides the support system which the student needs for this creativity.

The Theological Principle of "Salvation History"

During the past generation, certain scholars have developed a type of theological thought which they have called "salvation history." These theologians stress the belief that God has continued to work in the world through the historical process. Each day is not the duplication of a previous day but God is actively bringing about elements which are genuinely new in working out the divine purposes in history. We do not have to agree with all of the conclusions of the theologians of salvation history to appreciate the fact that God is working in the historical process.

We have our own personal salvation history. The recognition of this is as old as autobiography. It is a way of saying that there are significant events which happen in our lives which shape us.

The reality of salvation history is important for the supervisory task. The supervisor has his/her salvation history just as the student. They are at different places on that pilgrimage and they are not going to share the same pilgrimage. The supervisor must always be careful to distinguish between his/her salvation history and that of the student. The supervisor's task is to help the student keep that salvation history alive and vital and help him/her to be aware of the unfolding history. The supervisor may be a catalyst or a ballast when the student reaches a new threshhold of qualitative change in his/her salvation history.

The supervision will help the student examine his/her salvation history to see if there are patterns in the student's salvation history and what those patterns are. When they find those patterns, the student will be able to be more intentional in his/her ministry and behavior. The supervisor and student will also search for the meaning of the student's salvation history and project what that holds for the student's future.

The Theological Principle of "Revelation"

Christian theologians have said that God is a revealing God. While revelation has often been understood as propositional statements about God, theologians now speak freely of the divine-human encounter and the I-Thou relationship which the Christian experiences with God. This is the belief that there can be the presence of God within the context of human activity.

Revelation happens within the context of the supervisory relationship. The supervisor and student are not just about an undertaking that is human only; God is present. The supervisory task includes helping the student become sensitive to the presence of God in and among the relationships which occur. I recall a student who eloquently and knowledgeably defended propositional revelation but after two years of supervision said that he had experienced a higher revelation. It had come to him through the people with whom he was sharing his ministry.

The Theological Principle of the "Incarnation"

The incarnation is a central theological reality in the Christian religion. There are characteristics of the incarnation which are realities of good supervision.

First of all, the incarnation means "God with us" and open to us. The transcendence of God was not so absolute but that Jesus Christ could share the human pilgrimage and know what it is like to be one of us. The supervisor does not transcend the student in such a way that the supervisor is totally somewhere else. While the supervisor (hopefully) has a sense of direction that the student does not have and stands above the process enough to have perspective, the supervisor also shares in the student's hurts and frustrations.

In the incarnation, the Son of God made himself vulnerable to the human situation and that vulnerability led to the experience of rejection—even crucifixion. Directors of supervision often try to lessen supervisors' vulnerability, but a part of the reality of the supervisor-supervisee relationship is a certain vulnerability. The good supervisor must risk even the rejection of the student.

The incarnation modeled for the human race what whole and godly persons are to be like. There were limitations to the modeling. He was a first century man rather than a twentieth century person. He was a carpenter not a computer operator. Nevertheless, the modeling of humanity was an important part of the incarnation. Much supervision is done by modeling. We do not produce exact replicas through cloning but we do model discipleship, ministry and personhood.

The theology I have projected is mine and I do not expect theological consensus. However, I hope that I have shown a direct relationship between theology and functioning in the supervisory process both as a supervisor and as a student. The important element is the supervisor's self-consciousness about his/her theology and his/her function as a supervisor consistent with that theology. Obviously there is much more theology to be examined in relation to supervision than has been examined here.

FOOTNOTES
Chapter I

[1]Donald F. Beisswenger, Tjaard A. Hommes and Doran McCarty, ed., *Theological Field Education, A Collection of Key Resources,* Vol. I, Association for Theological Field Education, Berkeley, California, (June, 1977), p. 58.

[2]Charles R. Feilding, *Education for Ministry,* (Dayton, Ohio: American Association of Theological Schools, 1966), pp. 176-177.

[3]David Steere, "An Experiment in Supervisory Training," *The Journal of Pastoral Care,* December, 1969, p. 204.

[4]Beisswenger, Hommes and McCarty, *Theological Field Education,* p. 53.

[5]Ibid., p. 65.

[6]James D. Glasse, *Putting It Together In The Parish,* (Nashville/New York: Abingdon Press, 1972), p. 25.

[7]Ibid., p. 26.

[8]James Spicer, "The Place of Field Experience in Theological Education: Clues from Pastoral Theology," *The New Shape of Pastoral Theology,* ed. William B. Oglesby, (Nashville: Abingdon Press, 1969), p. 219.

[9]Glasse, *Putting It Together In The Parish,* p. 140.

[10]Feilding, *Education for Ministry,* p. 47.

[11]Charles Prestwood, *The New Breed of Clergy,* (Grand Rapids, Michigan: William B. Eerdmans Publishing Company, 1972), p. 33.

[12]Feilding, *Education for Ministry,* p. 15.

[13]Ibid., p. 27.

[14]Reuel Howe, "Theological Education and Ordination," *Making the Ministry Relevant,* ed. Hans Hoffman, (New York: Scribner and Sons, 1960), p. 133.

[15]James W. Bergland, "Field Education as Locus for Theological Reflection," *Theological Education,* Vol. V, No. 4 (Summer, 1969): p. 345.

[16]Feilding, *Education for Ministry,* p. 233.

[17]Allen Wheelis, "How People Change," *Commentary,* (May, 1969): p. 63.

[18]Glasse, *Putting It Together In The Parish,* p. 134.

[19]John 3:8 (RSV).

[20]*Journal of the Academy of Parish Clergy,* (April, 1971): pp. 63-64.

[21]*Journal of the Academy of Parish Clergy,*(March, 1975): pp. 43-44.

[22]*Readiness for Ministry* report book, Vols. I and II, (Vandalla, Ohio: Association of Theological Schools, 1975).

[23]Beisswenger, Hommes and McCarty, *Theological Field Education,* p. 86.

[24]Feilding, *Education for Ministry,* p. 15.

[25]Allen Wheelis, *Commentary,* p. 57.

[26]William C. Myers, "Process in a First-Year Pastoral Training Program," *Theological Education,* (Summer, 1969, Supplement 1): pp. 482-483.

[27]American Association of Theological Schools, *Voyage, Vision, Venture,* (American Association of Theological Schools: Dayton, Ohio, 1972).

[28]John J. Gleason, Jr., *Growing Up To God,* (Nashville/New York: Abingdon Press, 1975), p. 21.

[29]I recognize the exception to this principle in sub-atomic physics.

[30]John Hendrix and Lloyd Householder, ed., *The Equipping of Disciples,* (Nashville: Broadman Press, 1977), p. 41.

[31]Barton M. Lloyd, "Key Issues in the Personal Preparation of Clergy," *Theological Education,* (Summer, 1969, Supplement 1): p. 420.

[32]Feilding, *Education for Ministry,* pp. 149-172.

[33]Beisswenger, Hommes and McCarty, *Theological Field Education,* pp. 82-85.

[34]Mark 10:45 (KJV).

Chapter II
Developing a Program of Supervision

The director of supervision has the responsibility of developing a program of supervision in an educational institution. This responsibility ranges all the way from conceptualizing the program that will be needed to meet the school's goals to the implementation and evaluation of the program.

Conceptualizing the Program

The director needs to have a theory of education such as discussed in the previous chapter in order to conceptualize a program of supervision. Without a theory of education, the director can hardly develop an intentional program of legitimate, educational experiences which help reach the director's goals. When the directors have appropriate theories of education, they can feret out those programs which are educationally productive from those which are merely activity oriented. Because they have not had a conscious educational theory, directors have often used various activities as supervisory, field education or in-service guidance programs. Directors have sent deputation teams of students to churches over weekends to hold worship services, to take surveys or to lead in youth activities under the assumption that the young people doing these activities will benefit positively from such participation. However, students may be hurt rather than helped from such experiences. Even when these have the potential of being educational experiences, students will need help interpreting how these were helpful experiences. Student teams have gone out to a suburban situation on a weekend and reported back the next week about their grand experiences. The following weekend another team goes to a church in an entirely different sociological situation where there is not the opportunity for enthusiastic response. They return to the campus feeling as though they are failures because they are not able to match the grandiose reports of the team the week before. Team members have started ministry habits and patterns which are entirely inappropriate and continued them because there was no structure to make the activity a learning experience. Directors must work from a theory of education. They must see themselves as educators rather than a public relations person for the school.

The School's Goals

Every school has goals, some uniquely theirs and others which they share with education in general. When directors develop their programs, they need to do so on the basis of their school's goals. The school already set up its goals so that a director may start from that point and move toward the development of a program. The goals of the supervisory program will be related to the history of the school. Historically schools have certain ministry emphases. The school may be known for a particular expertise, so it will be important for a supervisory program to reflect that history.

The goals of a supervisory program also need to reflect the constituency of the school. A school has several publics such as denominational sponsorship, churches in the area, the community-at-large as well as the student body. The supervisory program of the school must reflect the needs of these publics. One or two of these publics may be so influential in the funding or operation of the school that the success of the supervisory program depends upon meeting their needs and having their blessing.

The goals of the supervisory program also must be in touch with the resources available. The resources are not only financial resources, as important as these are, but faculty members with appropriate skills, settings available and field ministers who will be good supervisors for students. As directors examine their school's goals, they can take the different parts of the school's programs and see how each of these school programs fulfill the particular goals. Directors will probably find that there are goals which other academic programs cannot meet that supervision will be able to meet and other goals of the school which are being partially met by programs but can be enhanced by the supervisory programs.

Since it is almost impossible to start off with a program in full bloom, a director of supervision needs to have in mind where the program should be in 10 years. Long-range planning will help to keep the direction of the program intact since every element of the program needs to be justified in light of whether it will help to reach the goals 10 years from now. This will save the director from going down some roads which seem expedient at the time but which in the long run will be dead end. Directors may face criticism from administrative and faculty members who point out the shortcomings of a supervisory program. Those shortcomings are bound to be found in a new supervisory program. Directors of supervision need to be in the position to point out that there are plans on the drawing board that will eliminate these drawbacks.

At times directors may feel that they are not doing as much as another school or that they are not doing as much as the director knows that they can do. If they have long-range plans, they know that they *will* do more. Long-range planning provides directors a way to develop programs logically and logistically sound while knowing that they do not have to feel guilty about not doing the best they can because that will come at a later stage.

Ten years is not a magical figure for long-range planning but that length of time gives directors opportunities to care for several needs. During a 10-year period, most institutions will have an accreditation self-study with an accompanying look at the curriculum. During such self-studies, directors can make input about the needs of supervised experiences. Ten years also gives an opportunity to evaluate what is happening in the programs and to do budgeting that will be adequate for the program and be realistic as a line item within the regular institutional budget.

A 10-year program needs to be broken down into the components which the program will need to make it work. Each component will need to have a financial support of the institution, the support of the faculty and administration and the support of congregations or agencies which will be needed to make each component of the program successful. The components in the program should be progressive so that they build upon the strengths of the previous components. As supervisors grow in their ability to do supervision, directors can devise more sophisticated components.

A Step-by-Step Approach

Develop Supervisory Skills

Directors may be skilled teachers and administrators but supervision requires additional skills and the reorienting of previous skills to the task of supervision. While many academic programs will help directors, there are no programs which are directly geared toward preparing a person to be a director of supervision. Notre Dame University and Boston Theological Institute provided an institute for directors of field education for several summers under the auspices of foundation funding. Midwestern Baptist Theological Seminary is developing a Center of Supervisory Training to assist people in gaining skills in supervising students, staff and volunteers.[1] Clinical pastoral education offers supervised experiences and those who continue in advanced CPE will have opportunities to learn supervision by supervising others. There is opportunity to be under supervision in such professional associations as the American Association of Pastoral Counselors and the American Association of Marriage and Family Counselors.

Selling Concepts

Directors need to begin selling the concepts of supervised

ministry in education while they are acquiring their own skills. Trying to sell the concepts before a director acquires skills in supervision is difficult because of the lack of believability in the director at that point. However, selling concepts is a continual thing, so directors should not wait until they have perfected all of the skills needed before they begin to sell the concepts.

Directors will usually find that they have to "sell" the concepts because of the threat factor of the supervised ministry. The faculty may be threatened because it is a new approach to education which they did not have the advantage of during their own training. It may be a threat to administrative people because of the uncertainty of what a new program will mean in the way of finances. It may be a threat to congregations where supervisees will be placed because they may fear losing some of their autonomy. The director may need to seek opportunities to present "white papers" on the subject of supervision. Directors may be able to point out the problems which the present system has in terms of not being able to get a student to integrate the material which they get in the classroom into functioning in a ministry situation. Many faculty members will have specific skills which will be helpful in supervised ministry so that the director can highlight these. By relating a supervised ministry program to goals, directors of supervision can point out how these concepts will help to meet the goals of the institution.

Getting Structural Changes

To have an adequate supervised ministry program, schools must provide adequate classes, adjunct personnel and academic credit to make them effective. Getting the structural changes will depend upon the ability of the director to sell the supervised ministry programs to faculties and administrations. Usually faculties and administrations accept programs such as supervised ministry to grow one step at a time. When the director demonstrates the value of each step, the school will be willing to take the next step.

Starting Programs

The programs must be realistic and not so grandiose that they are beyond the capabilities of the director and school to maintain. If a program is either overrun with students or has no students, the development of the program will be set back. Where there are students, there must also be supervisors and placements. The logistics of starting programs cannot be left to chance but there must be a matching of students, supervisors and placements along with whatever is required in the way of faculty, personnel and committees.

Evaluating Programs

There should be clear goals for the program. Those goals become the basis of evaluation of the programs' success. Evaulation should come from the director, students, supervisors, faculty and administration.

Mid-course Corrections

After program evaluations, changes should be made correcting the direction of programs, adding or subtracting modules of programs and making programs more sensitive to goals. The goals themselves may need to be changed at this point if they are unrealistic or if they are not adequate. The mid-course correction will be a time to use the information from evaluation to determine where you are on target with your plan.

Adding Programs

If there are long-range plans, the supervision programs will evolve from simple to complex programs. As new programs are added, directors must ask, "Is this the correct program to meet the goals; is the timing right for the addition of this program; will this program create or solve problems?" Conceptualizing programs is the responsibility of directors of supervision, but it is unwise for directors not to share this responsibility with others. Influential faculty members, faculty committees, and the dean of the institution need to share responsibility and give ideas about a supervised ministry program.

The Director of a Supervisory Program

Directors of supervisory programs are human beings who have their own pilgrimages. They have come from many backgrounds into supervision. Some have been professors in classical theological fields while others have been ministers in local congregations or denominational executives. Whatever the pilgrimage, the director brings a particular set of skills and a particular bias into the role as director of supervision.

Many people have asked the question, "What is the best background for a director of supervision?" There is no one pilgrimage which makes a successful director of supervised ministry. Certainly it is advantageous when the director has had advanced theological studies, experience as a congregational minister and experience in teaching a classical theological subject. However, when a person has succeeded in these areas, it is difficult to get such an achiever to change directions again and become the director of supervisory program.

Persons need specific training to be directors of supervision.

Academic institutions would not expect anyone to set up a program in their institution without some specialization in that area. Unfortunately it is difficult to find opportunities for formal training in ministry supervision.

The director of supervision needs an endless number of skills. He/she needs all of the skills of a congregational minister, of a theological professor and of a counselor as well as the specific skills in supervisory methodology. It is obvious that the fundamental skill that the director of supervision must have is the ability to supervise. Whether or not directors of supervision supervise students directly, they supervise the supervisors of the students as well as train those supervisors. Directors of supervision are more than administrators of programs, they are supervisors and trainers of supervisors.

Directors of supervision need to have ministry skills because they may need to teach ministry skills to students. Among those ministry skills is the "touch" of a minister where the minister is able to feel intuitively what the situation is. This is important for the director to have in order to be able to "feel along" with the ministry student. Directors also need to have good academic training. Directors do not look just at the functioning of their students but help them to get in touch with the theoretical base from which they are operating and the theological implications about what they are doing.

Directors need to have skills in psychology in order to understand the psychological implications about the behavior which they observe. They need to know about the processes of group dynamics in order to stimulate, control and evaluate inner actions of supervisors and students within groups. Directors need to have relational skills which will enable them to relate appropriately to students, supervisors, the faculty, members of congregations and the community. Directors must also have skills in organizational development because even if there is an organization present when a director begins, the organization will have to be adjusted or rebuilt every academic year.

The directors' relationships to their faculties are crucial for the success of a supervisory program. The director needs to be a member of the faculty. This means that a director should have the credentials to be accepted as a faculty member. The directors are not only administrators of programs but catalysts in an experiential teaching methodology. Directors may have administrative responsibilities such as finding placements for students, administering scholarship funds, and developing networks of supervisors and placements but beyond that directors are members of the teaching staff. Directors, faculty members, students and congregations should know the role of the director. Is the director a member of the faculty or the administrator? Unless educational institutions take seriously the role of directors of supervision, students, supervisors and congregations will not take supervision seriously.

Directors may find that they are loaded down with responsibilities either extraneous to their central task of supervision or superficially related to that task. What little energy is left for supervision has to go into basic administration of the program. Directors are teachers, not public relations officers, fund raisers, religious activities directors, therapists or counselors, or the denominational goodwill ambassador.

Supervision Settings

Ministry settings are necessities for a supervised ministry program. One of the main responsibilities of directors of supervisory programs is to provide ministry settings which will be learning situations for students.

Several types of supervisory settings can serve profitably for students. Concurrent supervision is one of these types. In concurrent supervisory setting, students are engaged in a program of supervision during the time that they are also doing academic studies. Student pastorates and staff positions may be concurrent settings. Concurrent supervisory settings have often appeared out of the reality of student employment by churches and church agencies rather than having been designed for educational purposes. Regardless of the feeling on the part of some academicians and supervisors that concurrent field supervision is not ideal, the reality is that in several denominations students will serve congregations while they are in school. The only question is whether these settings will or will not be profitable, positive and learning experiences.

Concurrent supervised settings give students some educational advantages. The classroom is not as artificial when students are in concurrent settings because the students become acquainted every week with the realities to which classroom theory is being addressed. This often raises learning readiness in students and helps them develop meaningful dialogues with their professors. It brings reality into the classroom so that the students can assist their peers. Concurrent supervision also enables students to take the ideas which appear in the classroom and test them out immediately. The concurrent setting is probably the best model for developing the socialization in ministry students who are going into congregational ministry. Concurrent supervision provides direct learning in a congregational setting rather than depending upon the student being able to transfer learning from a setting foreign to the congregation. The basic area of concern in concurrent supervision is usually with supervisors. Their time and energy is needed to lead congregations and the supervision of the students is an added drain on that. Congregational ministers have usually not been trained in how to supervise.

Another type of setting is block supervision. In block settings students interrupt their classroom work to serve in a supervised setting for a specific period of time. An example of block supervision is the year internship which some denominations require (such as the Lutheran vicarage year). Students have also done block placements in programs of urban training where the main trust has been social engineering rather than individualistic, clinical or ecclesiastical interests. Block settings may be year long internships, short periods of a few weeks, a summer clinical training program or a parish internship. The advantage of the block setting is that students do not have academic work competing for their time and they are completely immersed in the ministry task. This way the students learn about the demands of a ministry setting and can test out for themselves their functioning as a minister.

An important question about the block setting is "When should the student do a block placement?" Lutherans have used the year between the student's second and third year of seminary while others have made the internship year the fourth seminary year. Where the internship is the fourth year, the student can more easily make the transition from student to the profession of minister which helps with the problem of insertion in the ministry. Where the internship is between the second and third years of seminary, students are able to bring questions back to the seminary providing a new dimension and maturity in the seminary community.

Next to the training of supervisors, the most crucial task of a director of a supervised program is developing supervised settings. Many situations can seduce directors into approving less than optimum settings for learning. Directors may be tempted by friendships, denominational politics, seminary pressure, alumni and student pressure as well as the pressure of having to provide a large number of settings because of student enrollment.

The next paragraphs will provide a step-by-step approach to the development of a program of supervised ministry in relationship to settings. The director of a developing program needs to provide adequate lead time to accomplish these steps.

Obtain School Action

A school will need to take appropriate action setting up a

supervised ministry program. This is important beyond the fact that supervised ministry will be an official program of the school. Institutional approval develops consensus among faculty and administration with which the director can approach the students and the community from which the settings must be recruited. Directors who obtain school approval will have opportunities to inform the faculty about the discipline and educational goals of a supervised ministry program especially where the faculty has had the image of ministry programs being only to help students find employment.

Set Up Criteria for Supervised Settings

Directors need to set up criteria before developing field settings. The criteria should be based on the educational goals of the school and the ministry program. The criteria need to be idealistic enough so that everyone will know what an ideal supervised setting should be, but at the same time have the flexibility which will allow starting where the school and the community are. The criteria may be set on several different levels with a minimum criteria clearly stated. The director, the faculty, the administration and significant persons in supervised settings must recognize that the program is a developmental program so that the criteria used the first year will not be sufficient in future years. A school does not begin with an ideal program —assuming that there is such —but a program should be dynamic so that it is always moving toward better settings and methodology.

Recruit Supervised Ministry Settings

When criteria have been established, the director can go about securing supervised ministry settings. The job of getting supervised ministry settings is a recruiting job because ministers and congregations have to be sold on the idea that the school is serious about a ministry setting being important for learning. Some persons will be uncertain about whether or not they can do the job and will want to wait until others have tried. Ministers have legitimate reservations about whether this is the most productive place to invest their time.

It is important for directors to use the criteria established in recruiting supervised settings because strong and clear criteria will help avoid the pitfalls of pressure groups. It may help to have a supervised ministry committee who will serve as a supervised setting screening committee.

The question is, "Where do you begin in seeking ministry settings?"

You can send out a general mailing to congregations and agencies announcing the program and criteria and ask them to express their degree of interest. This has the disadvantage of getting responses from the wrong people. Competent people have so many demands upon their time that they often do not respond to local mail invitations.

Directors can go the elitist route and depend on their knowledge of satisfactory settings or those nominated by the faculty. They may also seek the counsel of denominational executives but when they do, the directors must take into account whether or not the denominational executive is aware of the educational goals of the supervisory program and will make suggestions compatible with the criteria.

There needs to be a clear understanding upon the part of the persons in potential supervised settings about the process of approving settings. Potential supervisors should understand that the school will not approve settings until a certain point in the process. The setting can withdraw any time up to that point and in fact should not make a commitment until that point has been reached. Both parties ought to decide their involvement together after orientation and supervisors' training.

Supervisor Orientation

Orientation should be a part of the recruiting and screening of supervised settngs. An orientation conference is the time to outline the philosophy of the school toward supervised ministry, the school's expectations and the general structure of supervision. The information and discussion from the orientation conference may alert some that they should not or cannot be in the program. A director may become aware that some who attend are not ready to undertake such a program.

Supervisor Training

Supervisor training differs from orientation. Orientation deals with the mechanics of the supervisory program whereas training helps potential supervisors acquire skills in supervision. Those who attend the supervisor's training will usually be the ones from the approvable supervisory settings.

The director should have screened out those persons and settings inappropriate so that the investment made by potential supervisors will be honored. The supervisor training is the final time of decision.

Institutional Approval

The congregation or agency should approve being a part of the supervised program and related to the educational institution. It would be advantageous, although not always possible, for the director to present the program to the congregation or agency and answer questions. Approval from the supervised setting is important even when there is no stipend.

Assignment

The assignment to a supervised setting is difficult and there are special problems involved in each school and denomination. The place to start is to have the supervisor in the ministry setting prepare a proposal which lists the ministry setting's expectations, opportunities, resources and information about the supervisor. While each school will have to work out its own process, it is important to match students' strengths and goals to the opportunities the settings can give to them. It may help for students to write out their goals so that the director can match them with the setting. Sometime during the process, the supervisor and student will want to have a conference to try out compatibility.

Students who have problems finding supervisors should discuss with the director whether the ministry is appropriate for them or what changes they will have to make before they can expect to be "a marketable commodity." This is especially an important conference for directors where there is little or no screening for entrance into the school other than having met academic requirements.

Convenant for Learning

The student and supervisor need to draw up a covenant for learning which will spell out the goals and relationships for the student in the setting. The director should have final approval of the covenant.

Student Orientation

There should be a two part orientation for students. First part will be on campus introducing students to the program and suggesting ways to make the most out of the program. The second orientation should be at the ministry setting and acquaint the student with the expectations and the setting.

Ritual of Initiation and Termination

It will help to have some ritual to introduce the student to the congregation or ministry setting and signal the beginning of the student's responsibility and accountability. Termination rites will also help to bring these to an appropriate close.

Changes of Assignments

Changes in supervised ministry settngs should be made nearly impossible, not only because of the logistics, but so that students learn that they have to live by commitments rather than running from them. When students want to change settings, they are often dealing with issues that make them feel uncomfortable and those may be issues with which they need to come to grips. If a student requests a change, he should write out the rationale for the change and give it to the director.

The director should only act upon a written request. The director's decision should come only after conferences with the supervisor and the student.

Evaluation

The evaluation process needs to be clear to all parties from the beginning. Evaluations need to be periodic as well as a final evaluation. There should also be evaluation of a supervisor and the supervised setting as well as the student. A director may do the evaluation or use a committee to help. The evaluations need to be according to the criteria which have been agreed upon.

The Recruiting and Training of Supervisors

Directors have no more important job than the recruiting and training of supervisors; it is the heart of their jobs. Supervised programs rise and fall on the quality of work done by the supervisors. Directors may get by with programs which are weak in other areas if they have strong supervisor recruitment and training.

Recruiting Supervisors

Directors have to start where they are rather than wishing and daydreaming that they had a large group of highly trained and experienced supervisors. That is an elusive dream which only becomes a reality after several years of training supervisors. One of the problems in reaching this goal is that when you get a cadre of supervisors trained, some of them will change positions, causing you to have to start all over again in training new supervisors to take their places.

You have to start where you are rather than where you wish to be. This is probably a good reason to begin with a few supervisors who have the basic criteria you are looking for and to whom you can give considerable attention. Even though you have to start where you are, you need to enlist the quality individuals who can grow into quality supervisors. Ruth Matarazzo gave some advice about training people in psychotherapy which is relevant for directors training people to be supervisors in supervised ministry:

Some of the important variables in effective teaching programs appear to be selection of psychologically healthy individuals and combined didactic and experiential training for a specific, well-defined goal. It appears that individuals who are already interpersonally sensitive and skillful can more quickly learn to become therapeutic. In most effective programs, the desired attitudes and behaviors have been defined; taught singly in some instances; and degree of skill measured, with subsequent feedback. Modeling by skilled therapists, peer observation and feedback seem to be effective and increasing student-therapist awareness of himself and motivating him to change.[2]

Even though you have to begin from the beginning in recruiting and training supervisors, you should find those who have good emotional health and ministry skills. Some ministers, however, are able to function successfully without being able to articulate reasons for their success. Directors will be better off to recruit those supervisors who understand why it is that they do what they do rather than the more dramatic ministers who are gaining greater attention.

It is interesting to me that some of baseball's best batting coaches never batted .300 in the major leagues. They were physically not the most talented players so that they had to learn the principles of hitting to stay competitive. This is a difference between hitting as an art and a science.

There are ministers who have the art for ministry but not the science for ministry. Good supervisors must have the art for ministry but what makes them good supervisors is that they also have an understanding of the science of ministry.

When recruiting supervisors, directors can let prospective supervisors know about the advantages which supervision will bring to their own ministry and person. Jervis Zimmerman, after supervising students for Yale Divinity School, wrote:

For me as a clergyman this has meant a recovery of many pastoral skills already acquired but sometimes neglected. It has helped me to stay alert in my ability to listen and to observe what others are saying and doing. It has been a continuing exercise in interpreting the significance of common behavior patterns through study of our students' responses. Always in these conferences we have tried to place the 'clinical data' in a pastoral and a theological perspective. It has helped me to deepen my insights into and understanding of the Christian ministry in general and my ministry in particular. It has been, I feel, a first-rate form of continuing education in the pastoral ministry.

Furthermore, the relationship with the program has been a lively intellectual stimulus. Here is incentive to read more, if only to keep abreast of our students and to enter intelligently with them into discussion of their reading.[3]

A supervisor of doctoral students told me that when he began supervising, he felt guilty about the time which he was taking from congregation responsibilities and often used his "day off" for his supervision responsibilities. He went on to say that later he realized that examining the ministry of the students had made him aware of his own ministry processes. It had sharpened his own ministry so that his congregation was gaining because of his greater effectiveness rather than losing because of the time he took to be a supervisor.

When recruiting supervisors, you need to lay out before them—completely and above board—your expectations. Avoid hiding some of the responsiblities only to reveal them after potential supervisors have agreed to serve. On the other hand, directors can become so proud of their high standards that they overwhelm a prospective supervisor with the details of a program, failing to realize that the prospective supervisor does not have the perspective to see how all of the data fit together.

When looking for supervisors, directors need to have criteria. It is too much to expect that supervisors will already have supervisory skills for students, although they may have some skills in supervising staff people and volunteers. They need to have appropriate ministry skills to teach the level of students with which they will be dealing.

Another criteria is attitude. A person who is quite naive or cynical will not make a good supervisor. An attitude that is highly judgmental or rebellious will not be productive in supervision. The prospective supervisor must also share the goals which you have in the supervised program. If the goal of the prospective supervisor is to get some cheap labor, the person will not make a good supervisor. While we all have some parental feelings about students, if the goal of a prospective supervisor is to have the adoration or a son of a daughter in the ministry, the goal will hinder the supervisory process.

It is also an inappropriate goal for supervisors to want to create little images of themselves. The level of education will also be a criteria which a director must impose upon prospective supervisors.

The standard theological degree of a seminary should be the minimum requirement for a supervisor. There are certainly competent ministers who do not have the educational credentials which directors will look for in a potential supervisor. These ministers may have mastered the art of ministry, but they are less likely to have developed the science of ministry. It is unlikely that they will have developed the self-discipline to have adequate theological skills for the theological reflection expected in supervising ministry students. An exception to the requirement that a supervisor have a standard theological degree should be made only rarely and then when it can be completely justified to the whole group serving as supervisors. Supervisors also should have had enough experience to learn from experience and read experience.

Availability is an important issue in recruiting. Prospective supervisors may claim availability when it is obvious that they have such a heavy load that they will not be able to give the time to do supervision. On the other hand, many ministers can make the time available for supervision but fear that they will not be able to do so because they are unaccustomed to task supervision and do not know what will be required of them. You can help by assuring them that while the task is serious and important, it is not overwhelming.

When you are recruiting supervisors, inform them of the emphases of your program. Some ministers with a clinical background will believe that their role of supervisor will be that of a therapist when your emphasis is upon another aspect. More than likely many prospective supervisors will think that their role is more to acquaint students with organizations of a congregation and common ministry skills rather than an examination of the affective aspects of learning and theological reflection.

In recruiting supervisors, let them know what the students' needs are. While it may not be possible to let them know of the needs of an individual student they will be supervising, you can help them to recognize where students are in their general pilgrimage at your institution. This is important in recruiting because prospective supervisors may expect a far higher maturity level from students than is realistic. They may expect students to be far less knowledgable than they really are and thus be threatened by the level of sophistication which the student brings to the supervisory task.

As you recruit supervisors, you are not asking them to be lone rangers roping a maverick student, but you are asking them to join a supervisory team: professors, other students and other supervisors as well as the director. As a team member, they will not diagnose by themselves and/or act without realizing that they are part of a team from which they can get feedback about their diagnosis and their proposed action.

A part of the recruiting is to make clear what the policy of the school is with regard to remuneration. I have found that schools pay supervisors from nothing to $35.00 an hour. I expect more schools pay the former than the latter. While supervisors certainly can be compensated in ways other than financial, there is a kind of accountability that goes with financial remuneration which cannot be duplicated any other way.

Directors should invite prospective supervisors to an orientation meeting where they can learn about the mechanics of the supervisory program. This is not a training workshop, but orientation to give an overall view of the supervisory programs and the expectations of supervisors. There should be a contractual relationship between the school and the supervisors. This should be done in a non-threatening way because it is for the benefit of both the school and the supervisor. Such a supervisory covenant will lay out the expectations of the school, not only for the purposes of accountability but also for supervisors to know the limits of their responsibility and be able to look back upon the covenant from time to time to review what their responsibilities are in light of situations which arise.

The Training of Supervisors

Training is important to turn good ministers into effective supervisors. To accomplish this you must keep in mind your goals for training. The goals for training should correspond directly to your program goals, the goals of your institution and your philosophy of education. Samuel Southard, working with the training committee of the National Association of Musical Therapists writes:

> After consultation with staff members of the Institute in each of these disciplines, the director of professional services presented the committee with three purposes for the training: (1) to demonstrate the technical ability of a supervisor as a professional colleague to students; (2) to communicate counseling skills of the supervisor to students who wish a therapeutic relationship with patients; (3) to form and practice educational theories and techniques that cause students and supervisors to reflect upon the purpose and goals of their professional activity.[4]

Group training is important because it helps supervisors by providing them a support group in much the same way that supervisors will be providing a support group for students. George F. J. Lehner says:

> I have found it helpful in developing this TD (team development) trainer's design to view the participants as a temporary 'team' with a common (learning) goal and interdependent for the optimum utilization of their resources to achieve their goal. Treating participants as a team makes it possible for them to experience directly the process—and its consequences—which they might wish to utilize later, with whatever modifications they see appropriate, when they individually engage in TD.[5]

As you develop the support system of a team concept, you will be helping to develop the supervision of your supervisors in the future, inasmuch as they will learn the advantages of the team approach to supervision.

When training supervisors, you can ask them to do some things before they come which will enhance the worthwhileness of the training sessions. You may want them to read specific materials before they attend. These may include books or articles on supervision as well as a description of your own supervisory program. You should also ask them to write up one ministry incident to bring with them to be used in the supervisory session.

The supervisory training session itself should begin by getting acquainted and letting each share briefly about the pilgrimage. This should be followed by allowing persons to express their expectations about the training. This helps directors to understand at what level of understanding the supervisors in training are and how open they are to the agenda which the director has developed. It may be necessary for the director to change agenda based upon the expectations of the supervisors in training.

A large part of the supervisory conference will be giving theoretical input about supervision. This will include the theory behind supervision and how to perform the various tasks of supervision. The leader of the workshop will want to model a supervisory conference with a supervisor-in-training using a ministry write-up that the supervisor-in-training brought to the workshop. The leader of the workshop can follow up on this by breaking the supervisors-in-training up into dyads or triads and letting them hold a supervisory conference with each other. One session should be given where the first supervisor-in-training acts as a supervisor and the second supervisor-in-training acts as a supervisee.

Where you use the triads (rather than dyads) the third person is a process observer so that when the supervisor and supervisee complete their exercise, the third person makes observations concerning the process, dynamics, the body language, etc.

All of the supervisors-in-training will get together again after they have had the first such session for a debriefing by the workshop leader. After the debriefing, they will break up again to their dyads or triads and repeat the experience, this time switching roles. This is a way to test the didactic material which the workshop leader gives to them. It will help them feel more comfortable: they have already led a supervisory conference.

Below I have included the outline of a supervisor's training workshop which I held at Southeastern Baptist Theological Seminary.

Tuesday, November 8

10:00—10:15	Introductions
10:15—10:45	Expectations
10:45—11:45	How to hold a supervisory conference
11:45— 1:00	Lunch
1:00— 2:30	Modeling
3:00— 4:00	Meet with intern
4:00— 5:30	Write up meeting
5:30— 7:00	Dinner
7:00— 7:40	Triads
7:50— 8:30	Triads
8:30—9:15	Debrief

Wednesday, November 9

10:00—10:15	Where are we?
10:15—11:45	Philosophy of supervision
	Stages of supervision
	Knowing self and student
11:45— 1:00	Lunch
1:00— 2:30	Problems in supervision
	Issues of evaluation

During the training workshop the director will need to clarify the role of the supervisor in relationship to the student, the director and the school. Supervisors need to know the limits of their authority and responsibility as well as how they hold supervisees accountable and are themselves held accountable. The supervisors' training workshop also needs to provide the resources for the supervisors or to let the supervisors know where the resources are available. The training workshop is at best a general introduction to the art and science of supervision which will need to be augmented as specific situations arise.

One director of supervision with whom I discussed training said that he did not believe in training ministers to be supervisors because they were the professionals and it was a put down to them to talk about training. There is some truth and many problems in what this director said. It is true that ministers are the professionals in ministry and that they are the ones who have ministry skills, but it is a different thing for the ministers to carry out their performance of ministry skills and to focus those ministry skills on the task of supervising a student.

Supervising Supervisors

The job of directors is to supervise supervisors. The director's job is not to bring changes about in students but to bring changes about in supervisors in such a way that they bring about the changes within students. Directors should not take for granted that supervisors understand their task, responsibility, role and authority. Neither should the director take for granted that the supervisor will always follow up on the leads which they pick up in supervision.

The director should provide regular meetings for the supervisors to get together so that they can be a team and share together the supervisory process. This gives an opportunity for continued input about the supervisory process and develops a routine method of accountability. Whatever crises arise, the regular meeting assures that the director is not very far away from the crisis. Regular meetings also provide continuing education for the supervisors. Supervisors need stroking like anyone else and regular meetings offer the director an opportunity to do that stroking.

Supervisory Problems

Directors may be able to deal with many supervisory problems on a routine basis in workshops without dealing with a specific situation; however, many times the director has to take initiative toward the problems which a supervisor is having. A book could probably be written which would only detail the problems that directors have to face with their supervisors so that the paragraphs below should not be looked upon as exhaustive.

Supervisors may react defensively to students. It is possible that a supervisor has a general defensive reaction pattern but it may also be that a student hooks the defensiveness of the supervisor. Whenever supervisors are defensive, their effectiveness is minimal.

Supervisors may have problems with authority. It is understandable why they would feel uncomfortable exercising authority over a student when at best they have an adjunctive relationship to the school. Students may even challenge their authority which makes them even more reticent to assume authority. While some supervisors have exercised more authority than they should, the most prevalent problem is feeling comfortable exercising authority with a student.

Negativism is a supervisory problem. Students not only learn from being told they are wrong, they also learn from being told that they are right.

Confrontation is one of the most serious problems that directors have to face among their supervisors. Yet confrontation is central to the task of supervision. Students have to be confronted about what they are doing, the implications of what they are doing and the meaning of it.

There are times when supervisors are simply not supervising. They may be administrating programs, assigning tasks for the student to do, but are not doing the task of supervising. You assign students to supervisors in order for them to learn through supervision. If the supervisor is failing to supervise, there is no rationale for the student to be in that setting.

There is the danger that supervisors may try to become psychotherapists. The supervisors are to examine the behavior and functions of the student and to get the student to look at what is behind such behavior but the supervisor is not a therapist. Samuel Southard writes about the supervisor's identity as a teacher:

> Identification with *therapeutic teaching* rather than with therapy for the student was often an immediate test of the supervisor-student relationship. In a second interview one student asked the supervisor, 'Are you my therapist?' The supervisor replied that he did not see himself in the role of therapist and that he would discuss with the student those matters that grew out of the verbatim interviews and out of the work that the student would do as a chaplain. He would be glad to relate the interview through the student's own personality insofar as they would throw light upon his function as a minister. But he felt that prolonged discussion of personal problems should be reserved for the group therapy sessions that were being offered during the semester, or for personal counseling with a therapist of his choice.[6]

Supervisors create problems when they are only willing to deal with student's skill development. While skill development is a supervisory function, students need to get in touch with more than just the mechanics of the ministry. Supervisors often want to "straighten out" students' theology, ethics, or politics. The role of the supervisor is not didactic teaching but the examiniation of ministry. It is here that the supervisor may need to make reading assignments or suggest other ways that the student can get theoretical input.

There are serious problems whenever supervisors cannot keep confidences. The whole supervisory relationship is based on the integrity of confidences being kept. The general contract which the director should have with supervisors and students is that any material is open for the student, the supervisor and the director unless there is an agreement in a specific situation where it will be otherwise. At times, material should only be shared between the supervisor and the student. It will be a very rare occasion when there is material that should be shared only between the student and the director.

On occasions, supervisors make gross assignments for the student. This usually signals a frustrated professor rather than a field minister. These assignments may be reading assignments or handing in an overwhelming number of ministry experiences or writing assignments. The director's job is to give some guidelines concerning what supervisors can reasonably expect from students.

There are supervisors who fight the system. They want to do things their own way. They are professional ministers and they know what goes on in a church better than anyone in the ivory tower of the academic institution. On the other hand a serious problem with ministers is that they like to be "nice guys." Nice guys often become pushovers as supervisors. They find it difficult to confront; they let problems go by untouched; they do not want their students to be hurt and they want everybody to think well of them.

Supervisors (as well as professors) have been known to keep their students completely occupied with busy work. When this happens, the student has no time to do significant work that can be supervised and the student becomes angry at the insensitivity of the supervisor toward student needs.

All of us have a god complex to some degree. This gets in the way of supervision when a supervisor trys to create a student in his own image. A problem arises when supervisors fail to make the reports which the director requires. This is an avoidance of accountability so that the director has no way of assuring the faculty that quality is being maintained in the supervisory program. Supervisors may refuse to become team members. They signal this by failing to show up at the regular supervisors' meetings, not sending in reports or sending inadequate ones and by not fulfilling their expected role.

One of the most serious supervisory problems is that of the supervisory split. This is where a student tries to split apart the supervisor and the director. Students may represent to the director an erroneous picture of the problem he or she is having with the supervisor. The student may misrepresent to the supervisor the expectations of the director. This is one of the important reasons to have regular supervisory conferences because they cut down the opportunity for the supervisory split.

Evaluation of Supervisors

Supervisors should be evaluated, too. This will help them to know that they are neither completely off track nor perfect. A system of peer ratings among supervisors is a possibility among groups who are able to become well informed about the supervisory process of each supervisor. Students should be given the opportunity to evaluate their supervisors so that supervision becomes a mutual learning experience.

FOOTNOTES
Chapter II

[1]For further information, write Director of Supervision, Midwestern Baptist Theological Seminary, 5001 N. Oak, Kansas City, MO 64118.

[2]Ruth G. Matarazzo, "Factors Relevant to Teaching Psychotherapy and Evaluating Trainee Performance," University of Oregon Medical School.

[3]Jervis S. Zimmerman, "The View from the Field: A Supervising Pastor's Experience in the In-Parish Pastoral Studies Program," *Theological Education,* Vol. III, No. 3, Spring, 1967, p. 420.

[4]Samuel Southard, Th.D., "The Process of Student Supervision," Georgia Mental Health Institute, Atlanta, Georgia, 1971.

[5]George F.J. Lehner, "Team Development Trainer's Workshop," *Public Administration Review,* March/April, 1974, p. 124.

[6]Samuel Southard, "Criteria for Evaluating Supervisors-in-Training," *The Journal of Pastoral Care,* Vol. XVII, Winter, 1963, p. 199.

Chapter III
The Supervisory Setting As a Teaching Lab for Ministry

Supervision is most effective educationally when it is structured in an appropriate setting. A setting for supervision is defined as the placement of the student in a functioning environment which by its design or nature is capable of being a learning laboratory.

The Field Setting as a Learning Lab

Ministry education needs a laboratory just as zoology, biology and chemistry do. Where the zoology lab partners dissect frogs safely preserved in formaldehyde, supervision dissects experiences of living persons. The functioning and experience of students is the extension of those students so that supervisors and students can step back and look at a part of the students—that extension of themselves. Supervision can only happen where a person is functioning so that the person can be examined.

Students may learn theories about what they ought to do and memorize techniques for doing a task effectively, but when faced with functioning in a real, live performance situation students may not be able to "do" what they "know" to do. Teachers of driver's education in high schools are unsung heroes of our day. They take several weeks lecturing to students about state laws, about how a car operates and how to drive a car, but the moment of truth comes when they take the students out the first time and let one of them drive. One of my daughters brought home nightly reports of her driver's education teacher turning white, taking tranquilizers, cursing under his breath, screaming and getting leg cramps from pushing so hard on the floor of the car. No doubt teachers of driver's education know better than nearly anyone the hiatus between "knowing" and "doing." The supervision setting is the necessary bridge between knowing and functioning.

The transfer of learning is a major issue in the supervisory setting because the basis of supervision is that performance in a ministry setting enhances the learning process. The implication is that there is not an adequate transfer of learning from the lecture hall to the act of ministry. Supervision does not negate or minimize the cognitive, classroom education but seeks to make it more effective. While we have all known ministers who have not had the advantage of supervised learning who nevertheless became effective ministers, many of these are the most vocal for the development of a supervised ministry program. They found the transition from school to congregation to be difficult and the transference of classroom theory to ministry practice either minimal or very slow. If the transfer of learning from the classroom to the congregation is a problem, it will only be lessened —not eliminated —by supervised experience. While various settings of supervision will have different levels of effectiveness in helping the transfer of learning, much depends on the student. Students can short-circuit the transfer of learning by their resistance or can inhibit it by their own maturation process.

The socialization of the minister is a special part of the transference. Mark Rouch defines socialization as ". . . discovering and adjusting to its (i.e., job) demands, then implementing our self-concept in and through it."[1] The exposure to field ministry brings about that socialization which is in part the movement from classroom idealism to acting appropriately in the reality of ministry.

Because of the maturation of students, the learning readiness unfolds at different times in various students' lives. Learning readiness is developmental and while it cannot be externally forced, some procedures will help it happen.

This learning comes at the occasion of what Havighurst calls "the teachable moment." There is no magic formula to produce the teachable moment nor any way to guarantee learning readiness, but exposure to real ministry functioning and responsibility has been effective in helping the students' maturation process unfold.

The question arises, "Which supervised setting enhances this process?" Tom Klink lamented:

> Some students have profited from training in many different settings, while others have shown that no setting could 'lay a glove on them.' I have seen students thrive when assigned to two places, say, a church and a hospital; they seemed able to profit from the contrasting opportunities offered them. Other students founder when given similar opportunities . . . ."[2]

I have heard directors of field education, whose students take no major responsibility, report their frustration. They say their students return a few months after graduation asking for help in areas covered in the seminary curriculum. Leaders in continuing education report the same phenomenon. Ministers in continuing education programs most often request help in functions in which they were trained in seminary, but apparently did not assimilate the theory into function. The natural conclusion is that students have an increased learning readiness when they have had significant ministry to perform. This raises the importance of the supervised setting not just for the experience but for the classroom learning.

Some settings are more helpful than others for consciousness raising and creating learning readiness. While many factors are catalytic in the learning process, the most helpful setting is one in which there are experiences which raise in students' consciousness the issues they study in the classroom and with which the students know they will have to deal throughout their ministry.

If students who plan to be campus ministers are assigned to nursing homes for their supervised ministry setting, there are issues about campus ministry which will never be raised. Regardless of how good the supervision is in the nursing home, the minister's socialization will not be the same. However, cross-grained learning does occur. Students may learn psychodynamics in a mental hospital, for instance, which will help them to be alert about what is going on with persons later in a congregational setting.

A supervised setting does not just give students a supervisor but it provides a network of persons and relationships. Ekstein and Wallerstein described the psychiatric student's placement as a "clinical rhombus" which includes not only the student and supervisor but also the hospital administration.[3] The relationship is intricate inasmuch as all four parties are related to one another.

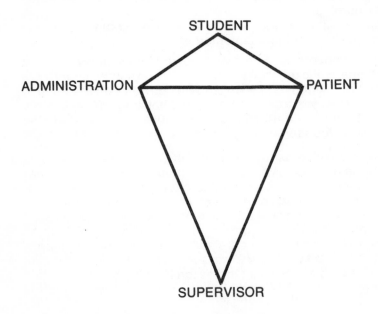

The supervisory network (clinical rhombus) is relevant where the setting is not a clinical one. The points of the network may be: student, supervisor, congregation and school. This is not an exact parallel to the clinical rhombus inasmuch as the interrelatedness of the parties involved is usually different.

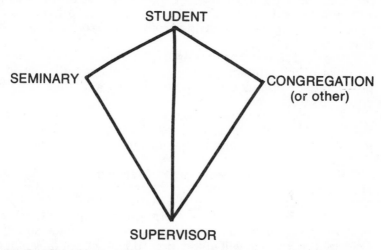

What is important, which the supervisory network points out, is that supervision is not a simplistic relationship between supervisor and supervisee. It takes place within a network or a system. Each part of the network is important and has demands which must be given attention. Each part can contribute to the supervisory task but they will do so from different perspectives, levels and intensities.

The productive supervised setting used as a teaching lab will give students opportunities for specific responsibilities as well as general observation. Students should not be just voyeurs upon the ministry of other persons because this would not test out their abilities and feelings. Students need to try their wings. On the other hand students should also become acquainted with a wide scope of church responsibilities so that they will not be unaware of the total perspective when they face the full responsibilities after graduation.

Hermann Morse says:

> . . . every aspect of education for the ministry needs to be brought to the test of its bearing upon the actual performance of that ministry, and that properly supervised and evaluated professional experience—'field work,' as it is here called—provides an experimental and testing laboratory which is of primary importance in professional education.[4]

Rewards for the Field Setting

Supervising students forces supervisors to examine more carefully their own functions and the principles by which they operate. Supervision pushes ministers to live by a stronger discipline than they might otherwise. They also have a feeling of professional esteem not only because they have an exalted place with reference to another professional but also because they have been recognized as having professional abilities from which students can profit.

The field setting has the services of a student. While the main purpose of the student's serving in a ministry setting is educational, most students bring stamina for work, enthusiasm, hope and ideas to the ministry setting.

The field setting also has the resources of the school available. Students bring a pipeline of resources to a field setting, including the school personnel, information, fellow students and literature.

People in the field setting get a sense of mission by having students serve with them. Regardless of how much students contribute to the field setting, the real reason they are assigned is for the field setting to make a contribution to them. Students are mission fields to which congregations can make significant contributions which will in the long run affect not only students but the people they later come in contact with. People in field settings will soon learn the excitement which professors have of molding and shaping the lives of youth.

The rewards for the field setting also pay dividends in the future. People will be interested in the destiny of the students and will watch their career. They will see the names of the students in publications after they graduate and take ministry responsibilities. They will follow the achievements of the young ministers through the years with a sense of pride that they contributed to the persons as students. They will realize that they had a part in preparing the ministers for their present achievements.

Criteria for Supervised Settings

Directors of supervision have difficulty developing supervised settings because they have students to place each year. However, directors can anticipate success in supervision only when there are criteria appropriate to the needs of the supervision program and students.

The critieria below have been drawn out of what I see as needs of ministry students. They are idealistic and I doubt that any one setting can meet all of these criteria.

The goals of students are as important as the specific criteria because some of the criteria may be absolutely necessary to meet their goals. Other criteria may not be as crucial. Regardless of how carefully directors place students in appropriate settings, there are some students whom it is nearly impossible to touch. Students can find ways to resist and avoid the benefits of supervised ministry regardless of how good the setting is.

1. The setting should provide competent supervision.

Supervision is the name of the game. Of all the criteria, supervision stands as the most important. Where there is no supervision or poor supervision, the student will not have a good learning experience, which is the purpose of supervised ministry. Regardless of the status of the supervisor, what matters is the job of supervision that a supervisor does to meet student needs. Some ministers are "successful" but cannot articulate why.

There are supervisors who have not kept up in their discipline. Other supervisors develop their own heavy agenda and fail to deal with the student's needs.

The competent supervisor is the central ingredient in the supervisory setting.

2. There should be the resources possible for the student to meet ministry and educational goals.

The student needs to be in a supervised setting with a covenant of learning which includes the expected ministry functions and educational goals. It is necessary for a supervised setting to have the resources available so that the student can meet these goals. If the setting does not have adequate resources, the setting is not appropriate.

3. The setting should allow supervisees to experience the full range of responsibilities they will face later.

It is important for students to "try on" their profession to see if it fits. The supervised setting is the appropriate place for that to happen. Even if there are settings available which are more dramatic or romantic, students need to test out their ministry career.

It is important for students to arrive at their first ministry responsibility with something more than hearsay knowledge. Students may have opportunities at other excellent and meaningful supervised experiences, but they need to become prepared for the ministry that they will do later. It is unthinkable that a medical school would tell medical students who are ready for an internship to take their little black bag down to the great cathedral in the city and check people with their thermometers and stethoscopes. It is not any more plausible if they tell them that one of the country's finest archbishops would give them personal supervision at the cathedral. There is no doubt that the interns would find many people frequenting the cathedral who need medical attention and that they might do some good by finding traces of previously undetected high blood pressure. However, the cathedral is not an adequate setting for the medical intern who needs to be able to use the many medical instruments and resources of the hospital and become familiar with the institution in which they will have such a great professional investment. It is altogether possible that an intern might profit greatly from a day a week in a public health setting at the cathedral, but it would not take the place of the professional setting of the hospital.

Ministry students may profit from excellent supervised settings outside of their area of career ministry but those will not take the place of settings where the students can confront the full range of ministry responsibilities they will face later. One important reason for ministry students to move out of the academic classroom is to get a model for ministry in their own ministry career rather than reaching the beginning of a career without having such a model in a disciplined setting.

4. Students need a supervised setting where they will be lifted out of their personal and ministry identity.

Students need to see who they are as Mr. or Mrs. citizen as well as being "Rev." When students serve in a non-ministry position, they are able to find out the importance of being an extension of the community of faith and their own sense of personal adequacy when stripped of their ministry identity. Ministry students are among the privileged class inasmuch as they have access to higher education whether by personal or family wealth, employment or scholarship grants. The students are also among the privileged class because they have native ability to succeed in academic matters. By the time students reach the point of higher education, they have developed personal identity which relies upon these resources. Students will gain understanding of themselves and their adequacy if they are separated from that identity for a time when they must rely upon the resources of their inner person rather than their academic framework.

One reason for this is to achieve what Klink and others have called "cross-grained" experience.[5] When students are required to respond differently from their usual response patterns, it widens their response patterns by making more responses available to them. It will also call to students' attention what their characteristic response patterns really are. Students may find the courage to try new responses in place of their inadequate responses.

5. The setting should provide students with decision-making roles.

Supervised settings should take students seriously enough to provide decision-making roles rather than making them errand runners. Unless students have significant roles, supervisors will not be able to see the students under the pressures of reality of decision-making. It is only with decision-making that students can "try on" the ministry.

6. Settings should be where students can help shape the destiny of people.

Students need to be able to see their own impact upon people. Supervisors need to be able to observe how students influence people and see the impact this makes upon their style and effectiveness. Students need to see how they relate to individuals at various levels and how they customarily respond to them. Students also need to see the same things as they relate to groups. Wherever there are people, there will be social structures which they create or inherit which in turn affect them. This makes it important for students to have an opportunity to understand and influence those structures. Supervisors will want to use students' activities at each of these levels to lead the students in self-examination and the examination of their role and effectiveness.

7. The supervised setting should provide financial support for students.

While it is helpful for students to be relieved of some of their financial burdens, it is also important for students to feel the dignity, the pressure and expectations which come with remuneration. Financial reward is a concrete way of projecting acceptance and rejection. Remuneration is another way to signal to students their significance in the task they are doing.

8. The setting should provide students with opportunities for initiating action and change.

Since success in ministry depends on a minister's ability to initiate action, ministry students need to have opportunities where this is encouraged and expected.

9. Supervised settings should provide opportunities for lay reflection.

Ministry students, as early as possible, need to make laypersons a part of their ministry team. Laypersons will always informally react to the minister's performance, so students need the advantage of formalizing lay responses to learn about themselves and how they are coming across.

10. Supervised settings should provide opportunities for peer reflection.

The supervisory period is an important time for students to develop professional identity and peer interdependence. Students will not always have professors and supervisors from whom they can learn, but they will always have peers.

11. The supervised setting should provide students with an experience marked by the dignity of service.

Students are feeling, human persons with needs to be

fulfilled. They need to have a sense of worthwhileness from their efforts and develop a sense of self-worth. Their supervised setting can provide these.

Few supervised settings will be able to meet all of these criteria. It may be more realistic to try to meet all of the student's needs by one significant supervised setting.

The Role of the Field Supervisor

The field supervisor —not the director —supervises students. While this seems simple enough, it is not as easily fulfilled. The temptation for the director of the supervised program is to try to supervise students through or in spite of the field supervisor. However, the job of the director is to supervise the supervisors, to prepare them to supervise the students. The field supervisor needs the dignity of supervising students rather than being the errand boy for the director.

Supervisors are usually much more closely in touch with the students than the director could ever be and therefore they are the necessary persons in the process.

Just as it is a temptation for the director to do an end run around the supervisor and supervise the student, it is a temptation for the supervisor to make an end run around the student and minister to those to whom the student is ministering. Supervisors should not look upon a student as one more person to whom to minister. Rather they are going to minister to one person (the student) who will in turn minister to several others who have been entrusted to the student's ministry.

The school, through the director of supervision, should have a covenant with the field supervisor about their responsibilities, goals and authorities. This sets the expectations out front where everybody can see them; it gives guidelines to supervisors so they know what is expected of them in being fulfilled and the student can know that there is no game playing going on with a hidden agenda.

The field supervisor represents the school, the setting, the profession and the student. The supervisor represents the school to the student and the ministry setting. Whatever expectations that the director and the school have, it is almost always necessary for the supervisors to represent these to the other parties involved. Many schools officially make supervisors a part of adjunct faculty.

The supervisor also represents the ministry setting to the school. Whatever problems arise, it is up to the supervisor to make them known to the director. The supervisor represents the student because from time to time the student has special needs. At other times, programs lay unrealistic expectations on the students and it is the supervisor who must represent the student.

The supervisor also represents the profession by modeling the profession for the student. The supervisor is a living, active and known example of the profession that students have an opportunity to observe thereby to become acquainted with the profession of ministry. The supervisor guides the entire process. Supervisors may request help from the director and fellow supervisors but they are the ones who are finally responsible for what happens or does not happen to the students.

Supervisors monitor students' contracts to see that they are meeting expectations. The director may be a third party on such a covenant of learning but the responsibility for monitoring the convenant belongs to the supervisor.

Also supervisors are the ones who are responsible for evaluation of the student. As evaluators, supervisors monitor the students' covenant of learning and make week to week observations which they feed back to the students. The supervisors are mirrors for the students to examine their ministry and see how they are doing. This is an important concept for the supervisor because it takes a burden off them. Supervisors are not gods laying truths upon the students, but supervisors hold mirrors before the students so the students can see themselves and change their behavioral patterns if they wish. Supervisors are not passive individuals who stand by and watch students do as they please, untouched. Nor should they "straighten students out" so that they do everything the way they are supposed to (i.e., the way the supervisor wants them to do it).

Supervisors need to make regular reports to the director of supervision. This is a discipline for them so that they will have to think through what is going on from time to time rather than moving out of habit. The director is ultimately responsible for the program and the only way the directors can fulfill their accountability is by having reports from supervisors.

The supervisor is an experiential theologian, with the responsibility for helping students determine the theological significance of the events around them. Their task is much more difficult than the classroom theologian because life is such a mixed bag whereas theology books have life all sorted out.

The supervisor is a climate-setter. As the authors of the book, *Elements of Police Supervision,* put it:

> He functions as a *climate-setter.* He sets the patterns of interaction for subordinates, influencing them by his example. If the supervisor is moody and uncommunicative, his subordinates will quite likely imitate him. Conversely, if he is cheerful and outgoing, these traits will be communicated to his men and be reflected in their attitudes.[6]

George Hunter says:

There are four key relationships in every field education program which need continuous appraisal and evaluation; these are not listed by priority because each relationship is vital if the seminarian is to have an effective field education experience. First, there is the relationship between the supervisor and the people who are part of the institution through which the supervisor serves; second, there is the relationship between the supervisor and the seminarian; third, there is the relationship of the seminarian and the supervisor to the people whom the seminarian serves; fourth, there is the relationship between the supervisor and the seminary.[7]

The Role of the Lay Committee

Laypeople are the final consumers of our services as ministers, therefore they are important ingredients in the training of ministers. Many authors have spoken of the hiatus between the pulpit and the pew, which underscores that the input of laypeople is an important one even if it is a difficult one to structure.

Lay training committees can be set up in congregations to be members of the supervisory team for students. People on lay committees are uncertain about what they can do and what they ought to do and therefore they are uncomfortable in the role. The director of a supervision program can help the lay committee by training them and preparing a booklet which explains their responsibilities. The effectiveness of the lay committee will be largely the responsibility of ministry students. When students are uncomfortable with lay committees, the lay committees hardly have an opportunity to function meaningfully. When students seek the assistance of the lay committees, the committees respond with helpful feedback and evaluation for the students.

Lay committees serve as another one of the mirrors which is held before the students, in order for the students to see themselves as a particular group of people sees them. This perspective differs from what they get from their supervisors, peers, professors or family. We may wonder which of these mirrors is the true mirror but the truth is that all of them bear truth to the students. They all reflect back to students the perceptions that different people have. The role of the lay committee is to provide a support system for the enrichment of the student. The lay committee is not an adversary of the student nor the director's "stooges" on the field, but they encourage the ministry students through complete and thorough evaluation from their perspective.

The make-up of the lay committee should be from a variety of backgrounds. The lay committee in a congregation and one in the hospital will be different in their make-up but both settings can offer a variety of vocational positions, ages and religious experiences. The lay committee will almost always be an *ad hoc* committee without any official representation of the institution. It is usually better for a lay committee to serve for one year. Beyond one year, the committee feels there is a recycling of their resources and motivation becomes more difficult. If a committee is needed for more than one year, a second committee can be appointed to bring in fresh perspectives. The committee must be able to keep confidential information.

The lay committees will need training. This may be done by the director visiting in the ministry setting or having a training conference for several lay committees. The ministry students themselves may be able to share the training of the lay committees. The students will have access to the expectations which the institution expects the lay committee to fulfill so that the students can have an orientation session for the lay committees. Without this training, the lay committees will feel uneasy about their role and will hesitate to take up the responsibilities.

The agenda for the lay committees needs to be carefully spelled out by the director of supervision to avoid misunderstanding. The lay committee can help ministry students develop their covenants for learning. They may already know the students so that they are able to give feedback about their needs. They are also able to verify that parts of the covenant for learning have been fulfilled.

The agenda for the lay committee is not only the mechanics of things such as the covenant for learning, but also the relationships which the ministry student has. These relationships may appear as they meet with the students as a committee. The lay committee will need to furnish reports to the director of supervision from time to time. These should be routine reports as well as special evaluative reports every six months or a year. These reports will be important for the director of supervision to match with other reports.

The Student's Role in the Field Setting

Students are the central persons in the supervised program, but they are seldom the central persons in the setting where they do their supervised ministry. The student has special relationships to the supervisor, congregational leaders and the congregation. These relationships need to be understood for there to be a profitable relationship marked with minimum game playing and conflict. The covenant of learning should define what the relationships will be (along with learning goals, etc.) with the supervisor and the structure within which students will be working. The covenant will delineate the responsibilities and the authority to carry out those responsibilities to that students will know for what they are accountable.

The roles of students in supervised ministry are roles of learning and service. To be consistent with the goals of an educational institution, the only reason for a school to be involved with a student in a supervised setting is for the setting to become a learning experience. The role of the student therefore is a role primarily as a student in the setting. This will require self-discipline on the part of students because there will be strong pressures in many settings for students to have service as their primary role.

Students under supervision need to realize that they will nearly always be under this tension. The problem is heightened where the students are in a tradition which allows and encourages them to become pastors in congregations while they are still in their college or seminary training program. In most of these instances congregations will look upon students as primarily ministers who perform tasks for the congregation which remunerates them. This kind of relationship is certainly a different kind than where students serve in specific student internships. However, even in these situations the students must not take themselves so seriously as to think that they have all of the pressures on them to produce the way that ministers have pressures who have had all of their professional training. The students cannot function the way they will be able to function when they finish their professional training and get experience.

The students should have appropriate humility to recognize that they are "student" ministers rather than professionally trained ministers.

One of the worst things that can happen to student ministers is for them to have a marked degree of success in a student pastorate so that they begin to think of themselves as professional ministers rather than student ministers. This freezes their depth of sensitivity, learning, understanding and growth at the student level.

Service is also a part of the student's role in a supervised ministry setting. Students deserve the dignity of knowing that they are helping and making a positive contribution.

Students in supervised settings belong to ministry teams. Senior ministers of congregations as well as laypeople are members of the ministry team who need to be recognized as such by the student. Students do not move into a setting to do "their thing" for a semester or a year; they join the team. In fact, team work is important for supervision to be effective. Joe Gross' analogy of pastoral supervision is that of the two man railroad push cart. He says:

> Standing face to face and each pushing on his side of the handle, the energy is transmitted into the gearbox located in the fulcrum and creates the momentum for the cart to go down the tracks. Supervision, it seems to me, is like an experienced push cart operator teaching a new employee how to best push the handle for maximum economy.[8]

Unless students are willing to become team members, they may destroy more than they construct. The destruction relates to their own development as well as the setting.

Students in supervision face the tension of moving back and forth from the role of a student to the role of the minister. They may not always be certain whether the supervisor is calling upon them to do a certain task because they are a student or a minister. They may not be sure whether in a particular situation if the congregation perceives them as student or minister. At times, supervisors can help by clarifying what role students will be serving in. In some situations, however, students will have to function with that ambiguity. However, that is a learning experience because all through their ministry they will have to examine whether their authority is being perceived as personal authority, ministerial authority or institutional authority.

Problems Which Arise in the Ministry Setting

There is no way to enumerate all of the problems which can arise in ministry settings, but some happen with regularity.

One common problem is that the supervisor in the ministry setting gives too much or too little responsibility to the supervisee. Where too much responsibility is given, the supervisees can be overwhelmed and anxiety or depression will interfere with the learning process.

Where there is too little responsibility for supervisees, they will likely react in one of two ways. They will see that they are not being taken seriously and therefore they will not take their ministry or their learning tasks seriously. Their second reaction may be that of anger, since they had anticipated this being a significant learning experience. They are struggling toward adulthood, and when they are given small responsibilities it reinforces their feelings of adolescence rather than their adulthood. The amount of responsibility put upon the supervisees will signal how seriously people take students. Supervisors may lay false expectations on the students by giving students all of the jobs which they do not want to do. Such assignments are not only poor supervisory process but it is also bad supervisory modeling.

Another problem which arises is conflict among persons in the setting. The conflict need not be related directly to the student's presence for the student to be affected by it. While the student may gain some insight and skills in conflict management, these may not have been the student's goals. Field supervisors may find their time and energy so taken up in dealing with the conflict that they have little time to supervise the students.

Crises may arise in the ministry setting. The supervisor may leave the ministry setting which directly creates a problem for supervisees. There are other crises such as death, tragedy, financial problems, legal problems, fires or storms. While many of these crises give opportunity for serendipity supervisory experiences, most often the supervisor and others are rushing past the needs of the supervisees to put out the fires which the crisis has brought.

Students create problems in ministry settings, too. After they see the way a ministry setting functions, they may want a different task than the one they agreed on. Not only have they agreed to a covenant with regard to a particular task, but the setting has made its plans around the fact that the student would be functioning in a specific task. The student may even want to change settings because of conflict with the supervisor or others or because the student believes that the grass is greener on the other side. It is important for students to learn that it is possible to get a bad deal in life so that they should look at each situation very carefully before they begin. If the director lets students off the hook during their supervision, they may reinforce trying to answer every problem which arises by being a spiritual gypsy.

Students do have conflicts with members of the congregations just as professional ministers do. This creates a special problem with students. Since the students will be gone in a short time, if they do not see that they have anything to lose and feel that it is important for them to straighten people or organizations out, they may lash out in immaturity. Supervisors do have some clout in situations like this because there is a covenant of learning and there is also an academic grade. Along with that, there may be a difference in the perception of students and people in the ministry setting about what is appropriate behavior for students. This may include students' dating habits, actions toward families, dress, language or personal habits.

The basic problem boils down to whether or not students can keep their covenants or not. If there is an adequate covenant of learning, the supervisor has an instrument to help both students and the ministry setting through the problems which arise.

FOOTNOTES
Chapter III

[1]Mark Rouch, *Competent Ministry,* (Nashville/New York: Abingdon Press, 1974), p. 108.

[2]Charles R. Feilding, *Education for Ministry,* (Dayton, Ohio: American Association of Theological Schools, 1966), p. 209.

[3]Rudolf Ekstein and Robert S. Wallerstein, *Teaching and Learning of Psychotherapy,* (New York: International Universities Press, Rev. 1972).

[4]J. Christy Wilson, ed., *Ministers in Training,* (Princeton, New Jersey: The Directors of Field Work in the Theological Seminaries of the Presbyterian Church, USA, 1957), p. 27.

[5]Feilding, *Education for Ministry,* p. 191f.

[6]William B. Melnicoe and Jan Mennig, *Elements of Police Supervision,* (Beverly Hills, California: Glencoe Press, 1969), p. 35.

[7]George I. Hunter Jr. and Ruth Deraney Khiralla, *Supervised Field Education Training Manual,* (Cambridge, Massachusetts: Episcopal Theological School, Rev. 1973), p. 11.

[8]Donald F. Beisswenger, Tjaard A. Hommes and Doran McCarty, ed., *Theological Field Education, A Collection of Key Resources,* Vol. I, Association for Theological Field Education, Berkeley, California, (June, 1977), p. 65.

Supervising Students in Ministry

Supervising students is an important and awesome responsibility. Supervisors are the models students see, the teachers students feel free to question and the resource readily available.

The Job of the Supervisor

Socrates saw philosophers as the midwives of truth. Supervisors are the midwives of persons who are becoming their full potential selves. Supervisors help students to fulfill their God-given and God-intended capacities and calling. Supervisors are not necessarily to create ministers out of students. In fact one important function of supervisors is to help the students clarify their call to ministry. It is a very important job of a supervisor to help students clarify that they should *not* be in ministry when they are erroneously entering the ministry. The supervisor may save students years of wasted preparation and frustration, help them move toward what their goals really should be without having faced failure in the ministry and help them avoid the guilt which many have faced when they made the transition.

Recognizing that part of the job of supervisors is to help students struggle through the issue of whether they ought to be in the ministry or not, an important task of supervisors is to help students gain a ministry identity and the skills and understanding appropriate to the ministry. Supervisors are not therapists; they are ministers. They are ministers who are shining the spotlights of their experience on various areas of ministry so that students can see the rocks and the shallows upon which they can wreck their ships of ministry and take them through the channels safely.

Supervisors are sensitive to the hurts, needs and sufferings of the students and know how to make students aware of that sensitivity. The supervisors may need to direct students toward therapy but their role is that of a minister although at times that ministry may need to be directed toward the student. The supervisors are administrators who must exercise authority and leadership toward students, the systems of supervision and the supervised setting. As administrators, the supervisors need to keep records, hold meetings, establish priorities and plan for themselves and the students.

The job of a supervisor also includes being a theological teacher. While they are not the "stand up and lecture" professors for the students, supervisors help students to see the theological meaning in what is happening to them in their ministry. The supervisor also develops an intentional ministry based on a theological foundation. Good supervisors are able to articulate these principles for the students and then show how the principles work out in the lives of people and in institutions.

Styles of Supervision

What is the Focus of Supervision?

Earlier I have referred to the three approaches to the educative task. These approaches become important to developing of supervision because your focus on an educative task will determine what types of supervision are adequate and appropriate. If the focus of supervision is upon the cognitive approach to learning, the supervisory task will be related to the more traditional didactic model. If the focus of the supervision is upon the task of skill learning, there are other models which will help students to learn and practice mechanical skills. However, when the focus of supervision is upon the development of the affective and personhood issues, a new range of types of supervision will be needed.

Models of Supervision

Several different models of supervision are readily recognizable and each of these types has a function at the right time and the right place. One of these is not "the" type that a supervisor should use, but supervisors should examine the situation and see which type is called for.

First, there is the model of supervision in industry where a foreman oversees production. Foremen coordinate the production lines to get people to do their job in order to meet quotas.

A second model is in business where a boss apportions work to various employees, sets deadlines and answers questions which may be beyond the scope of a particular employee's responsibility.

Third, there is the army type of supervision most usually characterized by the sergeant who gives commands to which people respond unthinkingly.

Fourth, there is also supervision within a craft where a master craftsman shows apprentices how to do certain tasks and watches while they learn.

A fifth model of supervision is the penal model, where there is a warden and guards who keep prisoners in line and keep them obeying the rules.

A sixth model of supervision is seen in an orchestra where a director keeps all of the musicians on pitch and in time, reaching a common goal by coordinating their efforts.

A seventh kind of supervision can be seen in the academic community where a teacher gives didactic material, expects students to do special projects and to be able to repeat material learned during the course of study.

An eighth model is in the medical profession where the supervision is clinical. Here medical supervisors go over cases of illnesses with the fledgling physicians to inform them and to check out how they are functioning.

A ninth model of supervision is in marriage where the husband and wife share mutuality. Marriage may not often be thought of as supervisory but let one of the marriage partners not show up at home some night and see if there is not some supervision by the other partner the next day. Supervision within marriage is a mutual supervision in relationship to the roles to which they consciously or unconsciously agree.

The last type of supervision is that which happens in a family where a parent supervises children. During the first few years, there is constant, close and intensive supervision of the children while later parents offer more freedom for the children to act.

Approaches to Supervision in Supervised Ministry

One approach in supervised ministry is the block placement. This is where a student leaves the campus and goes to a ministry setting for a block of time independent of seminary studies. This is the equivalent of an intern year off-campus.

Concurrent supervision is where students are related to ministry settings at the same time that they are regularly enrolled in a school. While concurrent placements compete for student's time, they also allow students to immediately test out ideas that they learn in the classroom.

Self-supervision is where students seek out the persons who have expertise in a particular area in which they need assistance. They are expected to get the help they need, but they are left to themselves as to what source that will be. This is much like life is outside of an educational institution where a person has to seek help from the experts.

Types of Supervision in Supervised Ministry

Don Beisswenger, director of field education at Vanderbilt University, lists seven modes of supervision in field education: work evaluation, instructor, apprentice, training, resource, consultative and spiritual guide.[1] Professor Beisswenger has given us helpful suggestions on which I wish to expand.

1. Work overseer.

The main responsibility of work overseers is to accomplish tasks. They define work responsibilities and attain the performance necessary in order to accomplish the tasks.

2. Work evaluator.

The work evaluator is less actively involved while supervisees do specific tasks but supervises by evaluating what they achieve. The task overseer is actively involved in the process but the work evaluator examines what has happened at the conclusion. Although work evaluators may be called in to examine the work while it is in progress they usually do not have direct responsibility for the production and performance but the evaluation of the performance at its conclusion.

3. Trainer.

The trainer assists the supervisee in developing skills and the socialization of a profession. The trainer may or may not be involved with the responsibility of the task itself according to the context of the setting.

4. Coordinator.

A coordinator in supervision pulls together the different supervisory resources to assist supervisees in their task of functioning and learning. Where there is coordinator type of supervision, it is a much more collaborative system where the coordinator works to get the system to mesh and takes an active involvement in the process only to budge certain parts of the system in order to accomplish the meshing effect.

5. Catalyst.

The catalyst tries to bring about change in supervisees by intervening in the process at specific and critical points. The style of a catalyst is to set the stage and let things run without being actively involved at close range and then to intervene at particularly critical points where there is openness to change or crises that provide special opportunities for change.

6. Change agent.

The change agent has much the same goal as the catalyst but goes about it in a more ordered manner. Change agents block out a specific course of action which they believe will bring about changes they want to see within supervisees. Whereas the catalyst works more charismatically, the change agent's intervention is more orchestrated.

7. Expert.

Supervision by the expert is the supervision by providing resources to supervisees. The expert has unusual gifts of knowledge and skills and is aware of multiple resources to provide for supervisees. Expert supervision is usually not a long term type of supervision but a shorter term, contracted supervision.

8. Consultant.

Supervision by consultants is a collaborative kind of supervision where the supervisees take initiative to get the assistance of the consultant to develop skills, solve problems, define issues and move toward goals. The role of the consultant begins by some initiative by the supervisee even if that initiative is only signing up for a specific course. Once that initiative has been taken, the consultant and the supervisee agree upon the role which the consultant will play and how active the consultant will be in the process.

Supervisors will operate basically out of these stances, but that does not exclude their functioning from a variety of stances. In general the most productive kind of supervision in supervised ministry will be the consultant.

Each type of supervision carries with it a different relationship between the supervisor and the supervisee. It is important for the supervisor to define what the relationships are in the different modes of supervision. There is a good possibility that there will be a difference of perception of the relationship on the part of the supervisor and the supervisee. One study that was made among social workers indicated the problem of the different perceptions of the relationship. The study reported:

> Whereas 60 percent of the supervisees saw the relationship with their supervisors as 'colleague-collaborator' and only 3 percent saw themselves as 'students,' 30 percent of the supervisors regarded themselves as 'colleague-collaborator' and 26 percent as 'teacher'. Supervisees apparently have a more egalitarian perception of the relationship than supervisors are willing to concede.[2]

There was also an interesting difference between perception of the supervisors and supervisees with regard to the supervisor's source of influence. This chart identifies those differences in perception.[3]

SOURCES OF SUPERVISORY POWER
AS PERCEIVED BY SUPERVISORS AND SUPERVISEES

Supervisor's Source of Influence with respect to Supervisee	As Perceived by Supervisors (percentage)	As Perceived by Supervisees (percentage)
Expert power	95.3	65.5
Positional power	2.6	21.1
Coercive power	.6	5.5
Reward power	.2	3.1
Referent (relationship) power	.6	2.1

The type of supervision is limited by the role which the supervisor is willing to assume, but it is also limited by the role which the supervisees will take. It is likewise limited by the perception which the supervisees have of the supervisory process.

Methods of Supervision

I identify three basic methods of supervision. The first is supervision by administration. This kind of supervision is carried on by administrative procedures such as setting personnel policy, creating a calendar when things are supposed to happen, setting guidelines for behavior and setting goals for action. Administrative supervision seeks to supervise in a painless way by handling everything in an impersonal manner and making the system one in which the supervisee interacts with mechanics.

A second method of supervision is reward supervision. Most often this reward is financial. Supervisees know whether they have done well or not when they find out whether the agency has funded their program for another year, funded for the same amount or given increased funds and whether they have received additional stipend or not. Again this method is impersonal. There is basically only one weapon in this supervisory arsenal and that is finances.

A third method of supervision is by supportiveness. The supervisor tries to build a support system around the supervisees so they can function in reality and still have a system which supports them when problems arise. It is a direct, personal approach to supervision which is also able to use a multiple means of supervisory mechanisms such as administrative procedure and finances. Of course, this third method of supervision is consistent with my definition of supervision as the provision of a support system for enrichment.

Times of Supervision

There are several times when supervision is likely to take place. The times of supervision are important because they need to coincide with the supervisee's learning readiness and emotional stress.

Crisis. Much supervision is done on a crisis basis. I have heard supervisors brag about telling their supervisees: "Whenever you have a problem, come to me." While supervisors should always be open to crises situations, supervision at that level only reenforces bad feelings toward supervision. It may even cause a supervisee who is hurting to create crises in order to get an audience with the supervisor.

Occasional. Occasional supervision is where the supervisor from time to time suggests a supervisory conference with the supervisee. Occasional supervision usually happens when the supervisor has some kind of agenda to place upon the supervisee or when the supervisors feel guilty because they have not met with their supervisees. The occasional supervisory conference will likely come after the supervisor has been asked for a report by the director of supervision or when something comes up that the supervisor wants to talk about.

Seasonal. Seasonal supervision is where supervisors recognize that there are special tasks which they need the help of the supervisee to perform. This may be to fill out the report to send to the director of supervised ministry, to work together on a seasonal task such as the church budget or Lenten services.

Project. Whenever there is a special project, the supervisor may call upon the supervisee to help plan and execute the project. The routine work of the supervisee may not be touched while the supervisor and supervisee work intently on a special project which they have to do. This project may be one assigned from the school or one which is inherent in the ministry setting.

Routine. Routine supervision is where the supervisors and supervisees set up a definite structure to examine the experience of the supervisees. This gives the supervisees the comfort of knowing that they can depend upon specific times to raise questions, express doubts and anxieties and get input. The supervisors have the comfort of knowing that there will be a way to be in touch regularly with the plans and work of the supervisees.[4]

Knowing Self and Student

The real power of supervision happens in the interface between supervisors and supervisees. This makes the relationship between the two an essential ingredient for what happens in the act of supervision. To be able to know what is happening, supervisors must know themselves and the supervisees.

Knowing Self

Supervisors must have OK feelings about themselves or they will create problems in the supervisory relationship. If they do not feel "OK" about themselves, they will not likely be able to help students feel "OK" about themselves. In fact, supervisors who feel "not OK" about themselves are likely to transmit an attitude of defeatism or anger to their supervisees. Poor attitudinal health is a virulent, contagious disease.

Personal identity. We are all in the struggle from adolesence to the various stages of adulthood. Whatever our personal identity, our recognition and acceptance of that identity is important for us to see how we relate to our supervisees.

My colleague, professor Roy Woodruff, believes that we tend to supervise others the way we were fathered. If that is so, knowledge of ourselves is not an incidental matter in supervision but it is a fundamental issue.

As supervisors we need to know where we are in our pilgrimage in life and faith. We have a particular history, heritage and future. All of these affect what happens on the interface between ourselves and our supervisees. The supervisory relationship is shaped by how long we have been in the ministry, our dreams and whether they are being fulfilled or frustrated.

Each person is a part of several communities. How we relate in those communities determines some of the relationships we have with our supervisees.

One community is our home. Whether it is one of fulfillment or frustration will likely affect our supervisory relationship and the questions we ask our supervisees.

We are also part of a church community and our perception of our success or failure there will color what we do with supervisees.

We are also part of a larger secular community. If we are part of a disenfranchised segment of the community, we will react differently than if we are power leaders.

We have a particular view toward the world in which we live. It may be sympathetic with the world or hostile toward the world. While theological issues are involved in whatever stance we take, supervisory issues are also tied up with it.

As supervisors we must know our own expectations, feelings, ego needs, and desire and capacity for growth. It is easy, for example, for our ego needs to get in the way of helping supervisees to become independent and self-sufficient. As long as we keep them dependent upon us, we fulfill some of our ego needs. When we continue to keep supervisees dependent, we have let our ego needs get in the way of our supervisory relationship.

Supervisors also have value systems. These differ from supervisor to supervisor but they are there within all of us, determining how seriously we take supervision and what we expect from others. The supervisees may have differing value systems.

Supervisors should recognize that they are contradictory in nature. We are not always consistent and all of our decisions do not follow a logical pattern. Recognizing that about ourselves will help us to sense what is going on within a supervisee and the difficulty that the supervisee has in understanding us.

Role identity. Supervisors have several roles and they must know about all of them if they are to know themselves completely. It is not always easy to distinguish between personal identity and role identity. This is especially true with the sex role, since so much personal identity is tied up with sexuality especially during the last half of the 20th century. The issue of such roles is a crucial one as a result of the growing consciousness among women about their status and roles. The reaction toward the woman's movement will affect the supervisory relationship toward all students, not just women. I recall hearing a supervisor ask the director not to assign a woman to him because if there was any way he could do it, he would not even have a woman as his secretary.

The supervisor also has a ministry role. The strength of the ministry role and the clearness with which the supervisor perceives it is important. As a supervisor models this, it becomes important to the supervisee. The supervisor who is uncomfortable in the ministry role will communicate that to the supervisee unconsciously as well as consciously.

The supervisor will also be in a position or job role. When supervisors are uncomfortable in their particular job role, they will not be stable enough in what they are doing to give concentrated effort to the supervisee. The supervisor also has a supervisor's role. Egalitarian and democratic ideas may erode the strength of that role. However, when misperceived, the supervisor's role may be seen as a license to practice psychotherapy or a temporary chattel mortgage with which the supervisor can threaten the supervisee.

Knowing the Supervisee

Every human is an enigma to every other human, but there are ways in which we can cut down the enigma. There are pieces of the puzzle which can be put together to help the supervisor. The supervisor can find out about the personal history of the students and learn about their educational backgrounds, their health and their families. Whenever supervisees seem to lack cooperation, it may be related to a health problem or family tensions. Supervisees might have experienced disappointments in relationships which make it difficult for them to relate to the present supervisors. All supervisees have their own pilgrimages, and they may or may not be aware of the influence of these pilgrimages.

Supervisors need to know their supervisees' goals in order to help them to achieve their goals. Where the goals are kept to themselves, the supervisor is often puzzled about what the supervisees are doing or not doing. Supervisors also need to know the supervisees' abilities. Supervisors can easily push the supervisees beyond what they are capable of doing or allow the supervisees to bad-mouth their abilities and get by with less than their real potential.

Supervisees have their own sets of ideas and these ideas will facilitate supervision or get in the way of the supervision. It is not only that supervisees have ideas, but it is also important how much those ideas mean to them. The supervisors may have the same ideas but not the same intense emotional identity with those ideas as the supervisees. Supervisees also have commitments which may be deeper or less intense than those of the supervisors. Until supervisors know where those commitments are, they will not be able to do an effective job.

Supervisees have self-perceptions. Supervisors need to help students see if these are realistic, grandiose or self-deprecating. Supervisees have relationships which are important to what goes on in supervision. These relationships may be with a member of the opposite sex, parents, peers or professors.

Knowing about oneself is a difficult and painful thing to put the students through and it is no less painful and difficult for supervisors. The effectiveness of supervisors, however, depends on knowing both about themselves and their supervisees.

The Stages of Supervision

Supervision is a dynamic process, always different from the day before. You never know exactly what to expect. Because supervision is intensely personal, it is subject to the different moods and stresses upon supervisors and supervisees even if many of those stresses come from outside their relationship and the ministry setting. The supervisory process is always moving and the movement should have a goal toward which it is guided rather than being random movement.

The supervisors and supervisees are both changing constantly. As supervisees gain competence, they are able to assume greater responsibility in the ministry setting. Each event, whether successful or a failure, changes the relationship between the supervisor and the supervisee. The relationship between the supervisor and the supervisee is a dynamic process: they have more or less trust; they learn to anticipate one another; and they become more helpful or more disinterested in one another.

All of these factors create the need for milestones. The stages, which are part of the process, give a frame of reference for the milestones. While these stages usually occur whether they are planned or not, the good supervisor needs to be conscious of them and use them.

The Initial Stage

The "initial stage" of supervision is the first chronological series of events in the supervisory process designed to be foundational for the main body of supervisory exercises. This stage is necessary whether the supervision is one-on-one or group. However, the number of people involved and their differences may affect the time it takes to move through this stage and influence the kinds of exercises used in the initial stage.

This initial stage is a period for the orientation of the supervisees. They will need to learn about the system in which they will be working. This may be an informal orientation but is no less an orientation. The supervisor and supervisee need to use this period to get acquainted. Although the relationship will grow, this is an important time for setting its tone.

One of the earliest exercises is for the supervisor and supervisee to share their pilgrimages and some of their dreams. While it helps if the supervisor has a life history or autobiographical statement from the supervisee before they ever meet, that does not supplant the need for sharing pilgrimages. The supervisees need to hear the recital of the pilgrimages of their supervisors. Often it is during such sharing that supervisees realize a sense of humanness in the supervisor and know that the supervisors have been where they, the students, now are.

The supervisors need to hear the supervisees recite their pilgrimages of faith and non-faith. Although the supervisor may have read the supervisee's life history, key signals come in the oral recitation which cannot be communicated in writing. Supervisees may voice emotions about the pilgrimage which escape the written document and the supervisors may ask questions during the recital. However, the supervisors should be cautious about questions and make the questions about date rather than probing into the psyche of the supervisees. The supervisors may be alert to different emphases in the oral and written accounts and check out later the significance of such differences. The supervisors and the supervisees will be working with each other through intense moments, crucial issues and personal conflicts so it is good that they begin with sharing the faith of each with one another.

At the beginning, the supervisees and supervisors may have a high anxiety level which is counter productive. No doubt such anxiety represents some reality which the supervisees will have to face many times in their ministry and therefore it is an appropriate learning situation. That anxiety should be called to attention and used (perhaps later) as a learning exercise. The supervisors, however, should determine whether the exploiting of the supervisees' anxiety is therapeutic for the supervisees or whether it is meeting the need of the supervisors to maintain an asymmetrical relationship. Ultimately the supervisees will function effectively as ministers only when they develop a comfort level—not necessarily anxiety free—but a freeing, comfort level.

This initial stage is also the time to develop openness, a two way street between two persons. Building the trust level is an ongoing process but the initial stage is important in developing an adequate level of trust to get on with the heart of supervision. Supervisees may find it difficult to make themselves vulnerable. Therefore it may be important for the supervisors to model this vulnerability and show trust in the supervisees. In many instances, vulnerability is real only because the supervisors are sharing their ministry settings with the supervisees and such vulnerability needs to be highlighted.

During the initial stage, supervisors need to set forth the expectations which the school has, which they have and which the people in the ministry settings have. This will include expectations of work level, lifestyle, reporting, behavior and grading.

The supervisees will have expectations too. The supervisors need to hear these not only out of fairness, but to gain clues about where the supervisees are, where they want to go and what they are willing to invest. These expectations and goals need to be formalized into a covenant for learning. This document will be important in later evaluation, planning the program of supervision and setting milestones for measuring progress.

Supervision, like any other activity, is subject to game playing. The supervisor will want to use the initial period to test out the "games" the supervisees play. The games may be called to their attention and they may even become a part of the covenant for learning for the supervisees to begin to relate straight across the board. Closely related to this are defense mechanisms. The supervisor may want to re-examine these from time to time to determine if they are still needed.

The initial stage is also a time to acquaint the supervisees with the ministry setting. The setting may have some dangerous aspects (prison, hospital, mental institution) which supervisees should know about, including what to do in an emergency. The setting may have some interpersonal booby traps about which the supervisees need to know. At times it is best to let the supervisees "stumble" into these, but in such cases someone without considerable maturity could get hurt. This might be the supervisees, someone in the institution, or the supervisor.

One of the most important tasks during the initial stage is to develop the covenant of learning. This sets the structural stage of supervision as a productive one. Developing the covenant of learning at this point is natural since this is a period of sharing of pilgrimages and dreams between supervisors and supervisees. It may take several sessions to work through the covenant of learning so that it is a solid base for the rest of the supervisory experience. When the covenant of learning is completed in written form, this will signal the end of the initial stage and the beginning of the next stage.

The Structural Stage

The structural stage of supervision is so named because it is the period where the supervision is consciously and formally structured. It is the stage when there is the main body of ministry exposure, routine review by the supervisors, interaction between the supervisors and supervisees and periodic evaluation. The main work of supervision is carried on during this period and it is the longest supervising period by design.

During this period, the supervisors develop the routine of the supervisory process. The supervisors begin carrying out the game plan which was arrived at during the initial stage. However, the supervisees also have a great burden of the responsibility for carrying out the game plan according to the contract for learning developed in the initial stage.

One important aspect of this period is reporting which the supervisees make. While doing ministry is important in itself, the real learning value will come when that ministry is adequately reported so that the supervisors (and peers) can help the supervisees reflect on their ministry. This reporting is the key difference between activity and learning, observation and supervision.

During the structural period, the supervisees develop knowledge, skills and competence. The supervisees will want to gain theoretical, practical and self-knowledge. They will want to develop skills which will be needed in later ministry and learn how to go about skill development. While a person grows in competence throughout life, the supervisees will want to develop a level of competence to make them marketable in the job market.

The team (supervisor-supervisee) can too easily deceive itself into thinking significant things are happening just because there is activity. Where there are pre-determined evaluation periods—milestones to measure progress—the team can adequately judge.

The central focus of these milestones is the contract for learning. The team can divide up the goals in the contract for learning so that they are met through certain functions and are evaluated at particular times. This means that there will be a process of ongoing evaluation. It will not be left to the last. The team can also renegotiate the contract for learning during this period. When the team evaluates, they will note that new areas have surfaced and others have seemed less crucial.

A growth cycle appears with each supervisory situation. For awhile activity goes in a more or less normal and routine fashion without any dramatically perceptive growth. This part of the cycle is often broken by a crises or a challenge when the supervisee has to struggle. However, the cycle returns to routine and has to run its course again.

Lynn Elder, professor of pastoral care, Golden Gate Theological Seminary, Mill Valley, California, remarked to me that the "teachable moment" is an elusive thing. We can never be sure when it is going to happen and it seems to happen in spite of what we do, yet we cannot really do anything to guarantee it. There is a lot of truth to that view of maturation and inspiration. However, all of us follow one methodology rather than another because we feel that it must do something to bring about learning that other methods do not. The supervisor (or supervisee) should not despair that every week's activity or supervisory conference is not a spine tingling experience. Many changes are more subtle. The team spends many weeks preparing for a few great teachable moments. Many changes happen and each member of the team is at a new place each week. Every week some attention needs to be given to where each person is.

The Termination Stage

The termination stage is the time to summarize and evaluate the previous process, progress and relationships with a view toward new relationships and responsibilities. This is a much neglected stage for several reasons. We often let the time of supervision draw to an end without having accomplished all we want and therefore try to wedge many last minute things into the final few weeks. We are also caught up emotionally in the ending of the relationship. When it has been a good one, we try to hold onto it by not giving attention to its process. Where it is a poor experience, we perhaps have already divorced ourselves emotionally before the final days. Sometimes it is just because supervisors are poor planners.

However, termination is very important to the supervisor, supervisee and the ministry setting. We all have emotional needs to be met by proper termination. The termination starts at the first meeting but we may not recognize it so easily then. We may not recognize the termination in the final days either and go on with business as usual because we have not covered all the agenda. We need the feeling of having tied up loose ends and brought something to a conclusion rather than having just quit.

The termination stage is the time for major evaluation. While limited evaluations have gone on during the structured stage, the final evaluation of the full supervisory process should be evaluated during the termination stage. If there has been a group together, the group should evaluate one another and the process. Whether the supervision is group or one-on-one, the supervisors should give their evaluation of each supervisee in writing and have a personal conference with each one. The supervisees should have an opportunity to evaluate the process and the supervisor. This should be a concluding evaluation and understood as such. From this time on the supervisor will no longer be evaluating the supervisee.

The termination of a relationship brings grief and it will only be understood as one understands the grief process. A significant relationship is being broken. Two or more people have tied themselves to each other and made a sometime troublesome and sometime triumphant pilgrimage. The supervisor and supervisee have developed some informal relationships that they have found meaningful and have perhaps learned to depend on. There may be guilt on the part of the supervisor for not having "done more" for the supervisee or guilt on the part of the supervisee for "letting the supervisor down." Supervisees may have developed some deep relationships in the ministry setting that they must now leave. They will sustain significant loss having to leave these people. The supervisees often invest deeply into the program, goals and dreams of the ministry setting. After giving themselves to these, they are now leaving them for others to do.

The termination period is one where the supervisor helps the supervisee work through the feelings of leaving the previous relationships. The old relationships are passing away and new relationships are beginning to develop. One of those changing relationships is with the ministry setting. The supervisees will no longer have an official role with the minstry setting. They may remain in the neighborhood and meet the people from the ministry setting but it will be a new relationship. They may even remain in the congregation but they will have a new status. The conscious effort of termination will help to signal this change of relationship.

There will be a new relationship between the supervisor and supervisee. Often they will be separated geographically as well as by function. Even if there is geographical proximity the supervisor and supervisee cannot remain in the same relationship. This period should signal the new relationship. The supervisor should raise to their consciousness what is about to happen and help set the tone for their future relationship.

The termination period should be the launching pad for the supervisees' future. During this period, they will have to face the future before them. The supervisors will help if they can show the supervisees the expectations others will have of them. The supervisees are no longer likely to be looked upon as learners, protected by that status. They suddenly will be expected to be mature, adult professionals. A colleague of mine took aside a recent graduate who was about to take a parish and told him in substance that his new parishioners were expecting him to be a mature professional man and not a seminary student. The termination period of supervision can help the supervisee make the transition from student expectations to professional expectations.

The supervisor can also help the supervisee become conscious of a new system of accountability and motivation. The accountability has been structured in the structural period either by the school or the supervisor. The supervisee will not likely have such routine and regular accountability from this point on but only when there is a crisis. Supervisees may be motivated by wanting to do well in classes and grades (at least pass) during their academic career. A new period of internal motivation is just beyond. Termination can help the supervisees prepare for that.

Related to this is student independence. They can depend on the initiative and instructions of others throughout the structural period unless there has been a conscious weaning process. Students will soon find that they must have independence and their own initiating ability. The supervisors need to lead supervisees toward this independence during the structural stage and continue the process during termination.

The supervisees need self-confidence as they move out of supervision. The supervisor not only should teach skills but instill a sense of self-confidence in the supervisees. This can be highlighted during the termination period.

Supervisors cannot just let the termination happen. They should mark the termination period on the calendar as they *begin* the supervisory process. Termination should be programmed as formally as filling out matriculation cards. There also should be a final rite of termination, a specific act at a particular time to signal that a significant transaction has taken place. Some have had a special meal in the supervisor's home or a restaurant. There have been significant prayer rites after appropriate discussion about what is happening. Groups have shared communion or a service of passing the peace. However it is done, everyone should feel that the process is complete.

Supervision: Examining Experiences and Its Data

I have already indicated that supervised ministry uses experiential learning. In supervised ministry, we hold up mirrors before the students so that they can see themselves as others reflect back to them. Supervised ministry is like mining experience where it is brought up for the assayer to examine.

In supervised ministry we begin by poring over living human documents. The question is, how do we get this experience out where we can examine it, since our basic task in supervised ministry is the examination of the ministry of the sudents?

By examining the data which we receive from the students, supervisors can find clues through the functioning of the students, see the patterns of their functioning, the consistency of the student's activities and the meaning involved in those activities. When supervisors examine experience, they are able to discover the levels of the skills, the kinds of attitudes and the depth or understanding of the students.

Observation

How do you go from experience to data to the examination of data?

One way is by observation. A supervisor sees students do their ministry and has the first-hand data to reflect upon with the supervisee. First-hand observation has some strengths. No other method sees exactly what happened, not a student's *perception* of what happened. Supervisors often do not have the opportunity or the luxury of direct observation of their supervisees in their regular work of ministry, but they do have the first-hand observation of them during their supervisory sessions. Students' behavior during supervisory sessions often will give clues as to why other people react to them the way they did. If nothing in the students' behavior with the supervisor is consistent with the report, then it is pertinent to ask why the students behave in one way among other people that they get such a reaction.

The direct observation of experience is not a perfect means, however. Whenever a supervisor is along, supervisees are bound to alter their behavior. Whenever students have to present their experiences by writing about them, another ingredient is added — their interpretation about what happened. That provides additional grist for the supervisory mill.

Another disadvantage of direct observation is that the supervisor may confront students about what they saw only for the students to set up a denial system by rejecting the supervisor's interpretation. This cannot happen when the report takes a written form, because the student has to stand with what is on the paper.

The Ministry Log

The ministry log, a journal of a student's ministry on a daily basis, provides the data of experience for the supervisor and supervisee to examine. The most effective daily log will provide the plans for the day, the actual activities, the writer's evaluation of the day and the writer's feelings about what happened (or did not happen). The ministry log will show patterns and meaningfulness of the student's ministry. Evaluations will show whether or not the student understands the dynamics of what is going on. The feelings show how much the students are reacting to the situations in their ministry, whether they are reacting to reality and whether the intensity of their reactions is appropriate.

Ministry Contacts

A ministry contact is a written report by a student about contact with a person which usually involves a ministry experience. There are several types of ministry contacts. Each type has advantages in particular kinds of situations which need to be reported.

The verbatim. The verbatim has become the standard instrument for reporting ministry experience largely because clinical pastoral education has used the verbatim so extensively. The first part of the verbatim is an introduction which gives the background material related to the ministry experience. This background material will include who is involved, significant data about the persons involved such as age and sex, significant situations (such as health, church membership, etc.), where the experience took place and under what conditions as well as the relationship between the minister and the persons involved.

The second part of the verbatim is the actual conversation as well as it can be remembered. Along with the actual conversation, the writers should put their feelings or thoughts which they had while the conversation was taking place. These are usually put in parenthesis after a particular recitation. The writer needs to differentiate between the various speakers and which recitation it is so that P1 would indicate the pastor's first recitation; P2, the pastor's second recitation; while J1 might indicate Joe's first recitation.

After the actual conversation are several concluding sections. The writer should evaluate what he thought went on and how he understood the situation. This should include what issue the writer detected. Another part of the conclusion is the theological issues which were raised in the experience. There should also be a section which deals with "Where do I go from here?"

The verbatim is an important form of reporting experience

because it gives words, actions and perspective. Supervisees may have difficulty at first with the verbatim form because they have to remember conversation but in a surprisingly short period of time they will find that they can do it. It will be important for the supervisor to hold the supervisees accountable for what they write rather that letting them "off the hook" by wanting to rewrite the verbatim after they begin the supervisory conversation. What they select to remember, consciously or unconsciously, is as important as what actually was written. What they select to remember will tell the supervisor as much about the students as anything they could have written.

Process notes. Process notes are the write-ups of what takes place in a situation over a period of time. They may actually be consecutive verbatims about one particular situation the student is experiencing. Process notes may be fully verbatim or move from verbatim to some other form. The process notes must be written up consecutively as the experiences take place rather than waiting until the supervisee has gone through a series of experiences. It is important for supervisees to write them up in order to see how they interpret the situation differently from time to time. It is also important for them to write their goals in one segment of the process notes to see later on how well they were able to fulfill them.

The process notes are good ways to find out how students are able to stick by a situation, follow through, demonstrate their intentionality and show their ability to make mid-course corrections appropriately.

Case study. A case study may also be the write-up of a situation which takes place over a long period of time but it is usually done at the terminal point in the situation or at least after a significant period of time. Supervisees will need to give a great deal of background material at the beginning of the case study. They will show the ebb and flow of the situation, the dynamics which took place among people in the situation, the various influences on the persons in the case study and the understanding and misunderstandings of the people in the case as the case unfolds.

Supervisees also may do a case study on an individual. This is much more like the medical model, an in-depth write-up about the history of the subject. A religious case history about an individual will go into the religious experiences as the individual remembers, understands and relates them as well as the supervisee's interpretation about the nature of those religious experiences. The supervisees will interpret the relationship between those experiences and reality and how those religious experiences affected behavior.

Case studies help students deal thoroughly with the incidents which take place around them and the people involved in their ministry. They show the perceptive ability of students with regard to a larger slice of life than more limited types of ministry contacts do. They demand a much more integrative type of examination of experience than more limited types of write-ups.

Significant incidents and critical incidents. Significant incidents are write-ups of events which had a special importance for the student. The significant incident write-up is not so much the presentation of facts as students' reactions to those facts. Significant incidents tend to be write-ups of events which were important life experiences to the supervisees rather than to their ministry to others. Supervisees may very well catch an insight or a special feeling in a non-ministry incident such as a date, a car wreck, the birth of a child.

The write-up of a critical incident parallels the significant incident except that it is a more crisis-oriented experience. The critical incident may have to do with the supervisee's personal life, health, marriage or family as well as vocation. As in the significant incident, the critical incident does not have to be written up in any special form but should be appropriate to the incident. The critical incident also is largely a supervisee's reaction to an event rather that the description of the event.

The significant and critical incidents are important ways for supervisors to see their supervisees' abilities to handle anxieties, their interpretations of what is important, their ability to react to reality appropriately and whether the crises of their supervisees are appropriate to their maturity level.

Electronic recording. Contemporary technology offers good opportunities for supervisees to share their experiences first-hand with their supervisors.

While the supervisors can see the supervisees' selective process in a write-up, there is a great advantage in having the supervisees' experiences recorded exactly as the supervisee was involved. The easiest way to get the supervisees' experiences electronically is by the use of cassette recorder. Supervisees can tape their sermons, other public meetings, committee meetings, counseling sessions and other ministry experiences.

There are pitfalls in electronically taping ministry experiences because of the matter of confidentiality. Whenever supervisees tape their experiences with a small group or an individual, they should have a clear contract about the fact that it is being taped, the use of the tape and the confidentiality which will be maintained. Taping can interfere with the supervisee's work and the response of the person or the persons with whom the supervisee is working. Whenever the taping is being done, supervisees are going to try to please the person who will be listening to the tape by following the supervisor's methodology rather than the supervisee's methodology.The persons with whom they are working are very likely to be more guarded and less open because of the taping process.

The best electronic means is the videotape because you not only hear the innuendoes of the voice, you also see the body language of the people involved. Whenever the videotape is used, supervisees will be confronted by exactly what they did and said, so that it is more difficult for them to "explain away" their actions. As in the case of the audio recording, there must be a clear contract made with all of the parties involved in the videotaping. Again, the videotaping may interfere with the dynamics of what goes on both from the standpoint of the supervisee and those involved in the supervisee's ministry. Whenever the videotape is used, the video recording should be done for a few minutes and played back for the persons to see so that they can become more comfortable with the process. This makes it as nonthreatening as possible.

One important thing is to notice the types of ministry contacts which students do. If they tend to use only one type, the supervisor should inquire as to the reason for not presenting other ministry experiences. Also the ministry contacts should reflect the kind of experiences which are being reported because some types of reporting are more appropriate for certain kinds of experiences.

The whole process of supervision rises or falls on the examination of experiences and data. Without ministry experiences supervision cannot happen. Neither can supervision happen where there is not adequate data about those experiences. Whenever supervisees get anxious to do ministry but resist presenting the data of those ministry experiences, they fail to meet a primary condition of making supervision happen.

The Supervisor's Responses

The supervisors will respond to the data which students present to them. Even an attempt not to respond will be perceived by the students as a response so it is important for supervisors to be conscious and intentional about their responses. Supervisors may use at least five categories of responses to the student's data.

Checking

First of all, they may want to check out whether they understand correctly what the supervisees are saying, how they felt in the situation and how they feel now. Supervisors do not want to approach the problem based upon a misunderstanding of what a supervisee is saying or the feelings involved in the ministry situation. When a supervisor and supervisee become confident that the supervisor understands the supervisee, they will be able to move on. Whenever the supervisor checks out the situation, supervisees feel that they have been heard, feel a new level of trust and are more willing to move on in an open fashion.

Probing[5]

Supervisors will need to probe to seek further information and to stimulate the supervisee to look further into the situation. Often a supervisor can push supervisees to see things which they have never been able to see before by the gentle nudge of probing questions related to the situation. The supervisor may want to ask the supervisees what they think was going on in the situation, what were other alternatives that people in the experience had or what were the pressures on those people.

Evaluation

Another response is evaluation. The supervisor will judge the appropriateness and the effectiveness of whatever the supervisees are doing. The supervisees will not learn from the situation unless the supervisor will make these evaluative judgments. Supervisees have anxieties because they know that the supervisors do make evaluative judgments and they will resent the supervisor who hides them. The judgments may very well be affirming judgments and therefore could help the students learn by a positive reinforcement.

Supervisors should not jump into the evaluation too soon. It is very likely that through the process of checking-out and probing, supervisors may lead the supervisees to make the evaluation which the supervisor would make. Therefore he can affirm the student in those perceptions without having to lay abrupt judgments upon them. Whenever the evaluations come too soon, the whole process of supervisory feedback is short-circuited. It is like giving away the plot of a play before the last act.

Instructive

A supervisor also needs to give an instructive response to the supervisory data. The supervisor is a teacher just as the professor on the campus is a teacher. The difference is that the supervisor begins instruction on the basis of the experience and the data from that experience, rather than from books. The supervisor needs to instruct the student about techniques of functioning in cases they present.

Supervisors will have different ways of doing that teaching; some will be more direct than others. The situation also determines the way the teaching takes form because at times, supervisors need to send supervisees back to their textbooks to see how they apply to their experiences. At other times the supervisor will want to have the supervisees engage in similar experiences so that they can see what happens when they use the new information which the supervisor affects them.

Support

Supervisors will want to give supportive responses to supervisee's data (which is consistent with my definition of supervision which includes the idea of developing a support system for the supervisee). The fact that a supervisor gives a studied response, even if it is a negative response, reassures the supervisees that the supervisors value. However, supervisors can do better than that; they can reassure supervisees that they have the support of the supervisor intellectually and emotionally.

There may be a sense of progression in these five kinds of responses but not necessarily. It may be important to check out data or how the supervisees feel as the supervisor goes along rather than that being the first response they make. They may want to return to probing after they have done some other work. Certainly the supportiveness must carry throughout the whole process. A benign suggestion made at the end turns into a saccharin ritual or a "marshmallow" rather than real supportiveness. Unless there has been a sense of supportiveness as the supervisor has gone along in the session, supervisees will not perceive the end supportive statement as anything but an attempt to rescue them after they have fallen on their faces.

The Supervisory Session

The supervisory session is the heart of the whole supervisory experience. The success of the supervisory experience stands or falls on what happens here. The experience of ministry is not enough by itself because students must be able to exact the meaningfulness of the experience and assess how they used their skills. The only way they will accomplish this satisfactorily will be through the supervisory session. The supervisor leads the supervisees through exercises that help them see what it is they did correctly and incorrectly and assess the meaning of what they did.

Having the supervisory session at a good time and a proper place will help make the session a good one. Supervisory sessions should meet at a routine time each week. Situations may demand moving the time but the most helpful thing would be to establish a time that is a ritual for the supervisees and the supervisor. The time of the meeting must be long enough to accomplish the agenda. For one supervisor and one supervisee, a minimum of one hour per week is needed. Where there is a group supervisory session, a longer time is needed to care for all the persons in the group, but that does not mean alloting one hour for each person in the group.

The place of the supervisory session is also important to its success. The issue is whether to have the supervisory session on the supervisor's turf or the supervisee's turf. Where it is held changes the dynamics of the meeting. If the meeting is held in the supervisor's office, this heightens the authority role of the supervisor. This may be counterproductive to openness in the student. Also the supervisory session should not be held where the supervisor and supervisees meet for other purposes. If staff meetings are held in the supervisor's office, there will be the bleeding of the feelings of the staff meeting into the supervisory session if they are also held in the supervisor's office. It is probably best to go to a neutral place where the supervisees and supervisor never meet for any formal purposes other than the supervisory session. When they go into that room and shut the door, they have signaled to one another that they are now in supervisory session —not in a staff meeting, a personal conversation, a coffee break or any other meeting.

The supervisory session begins with the supervisor's preparation before the meeting ever begins. Whenever a supervisor schedules a supervisory session, the supervisor should schedule 30 minutes before a supervisory session and 30 minutes after a session to do supervisor's homework. Before the supervisory session the supervisor should review what has been going on in the supervisory sessions and any data which the supervisees have sent. Just as a doctor reviews a patient's chart and a counselor reviews the notes made about the previous counseling sessions, supervisors should review the data which they have on their supervisees before each session. During this preparation, supervisors should decide what their goals will be in this particular session, what needs to be covered in the session and the priority items on the agenda.

The supervisor will want to accomplish more than there is time to achieve. Therefore some priorities should be set so that he is consciously in charge of what is being left out; otherwise they might leave out important issues while they deal with less important issues.

The supervisory session should begin with a ritual of mutuality. While the ritual of mutuality may appear to be a waste of time, psychologically there is a need for the ritual of mutuality (at least within our society) to feel one another out and to get a sense of commonality. This period should not last too long or it will be counterproductive. One of the ways to avoid difficult situations is to extend this period for several minutes so that they do not have to face the real issues. The length of this period will depend a great deal on the style of the supervisor and the comfort level of the supervisee.

The supervisor will want to review the agenda with the supervisee. This will give the supervisee a sense of comfort, knowing what is to transpire. This will also make the supervisory session more efficient because the supervisee knows that particular issues are coming up and will not have to interrupt the supervisor's agenda to bring up issues about which the supervisee has acute feelings.

The supervisor should ask for the supervisee's agenda. Supervisees may have some crisis with which the supervisor or the group needs to deal. This also gives the supervisor an opportunity to observe where the supervisee is with regard to perception of what is important. If the supervisees only bring up agenda which has to do with mechanics, the supervisor will know that the supervisee lacks perception or is trying to avoid substantive agenda. It is here that the supervisor will have to make some decisions about how much of the supervisee's agenda can be included in the supervisory session. The supervisor should be open to the supervisee's agenda and recognize that where the supervisee has great feelings, there are opportunities for supervisory issues. On the other hand the supervisor should have a general game plan which they follow to achieve results. That means that they must exercise care not to be sidetracked from what will bring those results.

In an individual conference, the supervisor will review the period since the last supervisory session. The supervisor will want to know how the supervisee felt about what went on and its meaningfulness. This is a period of accountability which will open up supervisory issues and also help the supervisor's comfort level because of the data which the supervisee gives. This will be especially true when the supervisee works in the supervisor's congregation or ministry setting and the supervisor feels a sense of responsibility to that ministry setting as well as to the supervisee. The same sense of accountability and comfort level will come from supervisees presenting their plans for the period ahead. This gives the supervisor an opportunity to evelute those plans to see if they are reasonable or if any of them would create serious problems for the supervisee or the institution.

Next the supervisor needs to review with the supervisees any of their special projects. These may be semester or year-long projects which the supervisees must fulfill or they may be projects to meet special needs which have arisen in the context of the supervision.

Attention should also be given to the supervisee's agenda. Discuss the supervisee's agenda before the main agenda of the supervisor. This gives supervisees an opportunity to get their data out when it is not influenced by discussing the ministry experience. Supervisees deserve the dignity of having their agenda attended to.

After these supervisory areas comes the supervisor's main agenda. This may be the examination and reflection upon a ministry contact, ministry log or a presentation by the supervisor or supervisee of a special need.

The supervisor may want to talk about other things besides a ministry experience. As such it should be separated from the discussion of the ministry experience so that one area does not lead into the other. The supervisor may help the student reflect upon some experience about which they are both familiar, because the supervisor sees an opportunity for learning and reflection.

After discussion of the ministry experience, preview the next supervisory meeting. This should include when and where the meeting will be held, and what the expectations are from the supervisee.

The supervisor has some post-supervisory session work. He should write up how the meeting went, his impressions, the issues brought by both the supervisor and supervisee, and the expectations and data for the next supervisory session.

The group supervisory sessions are similar to the individual supervisory sessions except that more needs are likely to surface and a mutuality must develop in the agenda process. Certainly the dynamics of a group are different from an individual supervisory session because there are several persons to interact.

The group supervisory session is likely to have these elements: (1) the pre-session work of the supervisor; (2) the ritual of mutuality; (3) the setting of agenda and contracting for the agenda of the session; (4) housekeeping items; (5) testing for crises; (6) the agenda of the day; (7) the view of the process; (8) planning for the next meeting.

Testing for crises probably needs some additional comment. Whenever supervisors meet with groups rather than individuals, they do not have the same intense kind of interaction which flushes out crises which have appeared or which are building. Therefore it is important to give supervisees an opportunity to surface any especially critical issues. Supervisees will often have some difficulty articulating crises; at best, they may give only a slight hint in a group session. Therefore it is important for supervisors to have "their ears on" to pick up and follow the slightest lead. It is a temptation to brush aside a supervisee's remark by calling it a joke or by saying that everybody has bad days, only to learn later that the supervisee faces a major crisis and was calling out for help.

Walter Telfer, formerly director of field education at Andover-Newton Theological Seminary, devised a work sheet by which a supervisor could determine how much time was spent on various supervisory tasks during the supervisory session. While this was designed to get supervisors to indicate the best distribution of the time in a supervisory session, it can also be used for supervisors to examine how they are using the time.

Foundations of Supervision

Worksheet on Supervisory Principles

Restructure the time by drawing solid line segments to show what you consider to be, in general, the best distribution of the Supervisory Principles in a 90 minute session. Place principle number in the proper segment.

Supervisory Principles

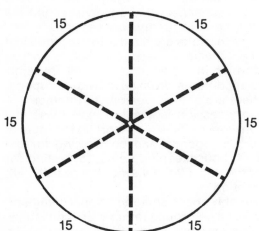

1. Humanizing

2. Data selection

3. Priority setting

4. Diagnosing

5. Reflecting

6. Directioning

90 Minute Session

However the supervisor does it, it will be important for the supervisor to examine what the process was during each supervisory session. This will begin to show the supervisor whether the supervisees are taking the initiative they ought to take, what kind of emphases continue to be made, and whether or not those emphases deserve to be made.

Problems Supervisors Face

Problems give supervision a touch of reality. Gemmologists polish stones by placing them inside a cylinder with other objects so that the stones are polished by bouncing off the various objects inside the cylinder. Supervision problems are like the objects inside the cylinder that polish the gem. The problems of supervision are the situations against which the supervisees react which brings about the polishing effect. However, whenever the problems are those of the supervisor, they can be devastating to the supervisee. It is then that problems become a hindrance to the process rather than being helpful to the process. These problems may be related to the system, the setting, goals, personal, interpersonal, conceptual or a part of the supervisory process itself. Problems in supervision are universal rather than being limited to those who supervise ministry students. In a book on supervision in the field of education more than three pages were needed to list the supervisory problems.[6] Another book on supervision in government and business also highlights a number of supervisory problems.[7]

Since there is no way to escape from problems, the healthiest approach is to recognize that they will be present and to identify them to keep them from getting in the way of the supervisory process.

Systemic

Supervisory problems often arise in the supervisor's relationship to the school. Supervisors may think, justly or unjustly, that they should have a freer hand in working with a student or greater input into the grading process of student's academic work. They may expect the institution to provide certain structures or materials which they believe will help the supervisory process. Conflict often arises within the supervisory system in student assignment. Where there is not a carefully worked out process of assigning students, chaos, anger and misunderstanding will arise.

Setting for Ministry

The problems in the ministry setting often relate to time, differing expectations and interpersonal relationships.

Supervisors may realize that their ministry requires so much of their time that they do not have time to give good supervision to students. On the other hand the time problem may be with the students, since they do not give as much time to the ministry setting as the supervisor had anticipated. One game that some students play is to tell the supervisor how much time they have to spend at the school, and to tell the school how much time the ministry setting demands. Since time and a lack of it will always be an issue with ministers, the supervisory process should examine the discipline with regard to time and the meaning of the various activities to which students give their time. Supervisors will also need to look at the importance of what they are doing and whether anything in their ministry is substantially more important than the education of the students they have under their supervision. There may be special seasons when supervisors do find that the time demands of students interfere with the special projects which the supervisors have to do in their own setting and this should be dealt with in a straightforward manner with the students and the director of the supervisory program.

Differing expectations may arise in the ministry setting about the role and work of students. The supervisor may have one set of expectations and members of the congregation another set of expectations. The supervisor may feel that the students are non-initiated fledglings while the members of the congregation expect them to be "ministers." Whenever there is a clear covenant of learning and when the congregation can participate in the supervisory process, the situation may be less acute; but regardless of what is said, there are many times when unconsciously there are expectations among the people in a congregation which differ with the expectations of the supervisor and student.

Interpersonal relationships often become a problem in the ministry setting. Students have new and fresh ideas which they believe should be accepted only to find that people within the congregation (and supervisors) are satisfied with the way things are and causing a breach in the relationship. Students may be abrasive or passive causing interpersonal difficulties. Students may not understand that the interpersonal difficulties may come because they are being used as a pawn in the hands of some person attempting to get back at the supervisor.

Goals

The expectations in supervision are very important for the supervisor and the students to understand. The reason why the covenant of learning is so important is that the instrument should point out the expectations clearly. Those expectations should be fair and challenging. A serious problem is where a supervisor expects a neophyte to function as an experienced minister. When this happens, the supervisor will likely lay upon the students responsibilities for which they are not prepared and fail to give them adequate support in terms of information and skill development to meet the responsibilities. However, it is also a serious supervisory problem when students are given work which is too insignificant. The students do not feel that they are making contributions, learning or involved in a project that is worthwhile. They will become discouraged and possibly angry. Since they have not been given adequate enough challenge, they will develop a lethargic response to what they are given to do and it may even result in a pattern of responses to ministry which will carry over into later ministry responsibilities. When that happens, supervision becomes a detriment to the students rather than helpful.

Personal Problems

Supervisors may have personal problems which create difficulties for being good supervisors. They may feel a strong sense of inadequacy as a supervisor. They may either be inadequate or they may feel inadequate when they are really adequate. Their inadequacy may not be from their inadequacy as a minister but because they do not know how to bring supervisory skills to bear on the supervisory process. They have been trained as ministers, not as supervisors. This makes it an important part of the director's job to give the supervisors adequate training for the job of supervision. Even when there has been adequate training, the supervisors may feel inadequate when they really have adequate skills for supervision. Feelings of inadequacy do not always mean that supervisors are inadequate.

Male chauvinism is a personal problem which is receiving more and more attention. Supervisors may not realize that they are creating different expectancies for the women they supervise than they do for the men they supervise. Because of prevalent patterns of ministry, the supervisors may not "hear" what a woman supervisee wants to get out of the supervisory process. When that happens, the supervisor will probably force the woman into a role which she does not choose and try to train her for functions which are more limited than she wishes for service in ministry. While I do not try to deal at length in this book with women in ministry, this issue is one of the most serious ones faced by supervisors of ministry students. An awakening of the feminine consciousness is creating new thrusts for women in ministry which in turn creates new frontiers in supervision. When supervising women in ministry today, supervisors must give careful attention to the agenda of the woman supervisee to see that they have compatible goals. Supervising a woman in ministry may not be just supervising another woman or supervising just another supervisee.

Supervisors have often needed to deal with their own god-complex. Their god-complex tends to make them try to act as an "answer man" because they feel that they have to fulfill the role of omniscience. Students can often force omniscience onto a supervisor by making them the "answer man." A god-complex may come out in omnipotence in which supervsiors feel that they cannot admit limitations or weaknesses and also feel that they must be powerful enough to rescue the students from whatever situation in which they find themselves. The god-complex also shows in the supervisor's attempt to be omnipresent and see everything that goes on with the student. The god-complex often shows itself as supervisors try to fulfill such roles as judge, reconciler and savior. Because of the god-complex the supervisor may not want any competition from others trying to supervise the students such as associate ministers or lay people.

Another problem that supervisors face is the need to rescue (which may not be totally unrelated to the god-complex). Supervisors may try to rescue the students from difficult situations and failure. While it is true that supervisors should be alert not to allow the students to be mortally wounded, the students are usually not so fragile but what they can take hard blows if they are in a context of supportiveness provided by the supervisor.

Prejudice is a problem of supervisors. Supervisors may have prejudice toward women, racial groups, lifestyles or theological stances. Whether or not the supervisors are overly prejudicial, wherever there are differences such as these, they need to be surfaced so that they can be honestly examined as to how they will affect the supervisory relationship.

The "problem child" is not only present within the family but is also a possibility within the supervisory relationship. Vandersal talks about the "problem child" in supervising in government and business and offers a process for dealing with "the problem child."[8] Supervisors of ministry students will also find that they have an occasional "problem child" and they will have to deal with the person. The temptation is to endure the time of the relationship and to short-circuit the "problem child" in such a way that the person does not cause major difficulties within the ministry setting. In such instances the students are not helped by their supervisory experience but have reenforced the pattern that if they cause enough trouble, nothing will be expected of them and they will be able to get by. It is here that the covenant of learning becomes important because the supervisor can keep calling the "problem child" back to the supervisory covenant of learning which is in black and white. Even here the students may try to play games with the supervisor and claim that they are fulfilling the covenant of learning. They may be correct as far as going through the motions of fulfilling the mechanics of the covenant of learning. When this happens, the supervisor may have to "put the bell on the cat" and let the supervisee know that he or she is being perceived as a "problem child" and if they do not learn how to modify their behavior, they will create problems in ministry instead of ministering to persons. The relationship will have to terminate if the student is short-circuiting the covenant of learning, but termination should come only as a last resort. When the director and supervisor meet with these students, they should hold the mirror up clearly before such students so that they see how they are being perceived. The students' defense mechanisms may be so strong they will not be able to accept the evaluation and when that is the case the director may wish to use other resources such as therapy to deal with the problem.

Interpersonal Relationships

Problems with interpersonal relationships between the supervisor and students often arise and sometimes these are not perceived to be problems. There will be an informal relationship between the supervisor and the students as well as the formal relationship. The informal relationship may be that of a father to a son, an older brother to a younger brother, an expert to a neophyte, a warden to a prisoner, a boss to an employee or some other. These informal relationships may get in the way of accomplishing supervision. However, the supervisor and students may feel comfortable in certain roles such as the father-son informal relationship role. Although they feel comfortable, it may not be the best role for the growth of the student. The student will not always have a father around to protect and coddle. One of the goals of students should be to grow up and become more of a peer with the supervisor, so it is important for students to examine their informal relationships from time to time and see what is going on in it.

Jealousy may arise in the supervisor causing a breakdown in the interpersonal relationship. The jealousy may come because of the success of the student or because the student is able to get close to some people in the ministry setting—sometimes closer than the supervisor is able to get.

Conceptual Problems

The basic conceptual problem in supervision is the theological stances of the supervisor and students. The supervisor may have a rigid theological stance and demand conformity from any student. Students may be messianic about a particular theological concept they have grown up with or have arrived at during their education. There may be conceptual differences also in the ideas about churchmanship. For example, the supervisor may be an autocratic leader whereas the students may be much more democratic or even laissez-faire in their approach to leadership style.

Supervisory Process

Problems in the supervisory process itself may create less productive supervision. For example, the supervisors may try to reproduce their own ministries rather than bring out the gifts which are within the students. A good supervisor will likely have strong opinions about what is good ministry, theology and scholarship. The supervisor need not leave these convictions but he does need to give the students the opportunity to develop themselves and their own style of ministry.

Confrontation which is inadequate or abusive remains one of the most difficult problems in the supervisory process. While there are supervisors who are abusive in their confrontation, the most prevalent problem with confrontation is that supervisors are uncomfortable with confronting. Supervisors like to be "nice guys" but non-confrontive supervision is usually non-supervision. Students need to be confronted about what they are doing so they will see what they are doing wrong or articulate what they are doing correctly. Students are going to be confronted by persons to whom they minister in the future, so they should have the opportuity during their supervision to learn that they can deal with confrontation. Many students have come from sheltered backgrounds where they have never been seriously confronted. They will not always live in that kind of emotional womb. Confrontation is very much like isometrics in physical exercise —when students push against confrontation, they grow their "ministry muscles."

A serious supervisory problem is when other agenda gets in the way of the supervisory process. The supervisor's agenda may be so strong that he fails to hear many of the things which the student is saying because the supervisor is hung up on one particular agenda item. This happens not only with inexperienced supervisors but with some with years of supervision. I recall an incident where one of the most famous persons in the pastoral care movement blocked out a student's agenda because of the particular institution where the student was ministering.

The very fact that the supervisor is trying to help a student may become a serious supervisory problem. We all like to help, but few of us have a feeling for what it is like to be on the other end of the helping process. Being a person who needs help has built-in possibilities of resistance so that supervisors can expect students to resist often when the supervisors are trying to give help. Social scientists have explored this problem thoroughly.[9]

Whenever the supervisor is unable to trust the students, there will be a serious problem. The inability to trust may or may not come from the actual behavior of the students. There are supervisors who do not believe that students can be trusted with significant activities and there are times when students' behavior creates that distrust. Whenever there is not a high trust level, there cannot be exchange and openness. Neither will supervisors feel that they can trust the students with enough significant ministry for the student to have a good learning experience.

One of the reasons why supervisors need to be supervised by the director is that the supervisors need some perspective about the problems which arise, some they may be conscious of and some they may not. Problems cannot be avoided, but they need to be recognized and dealt with as reality.

Games People Play in Supervision

Eric Berne and transactional analysis has made us aware of games that go on between people.[10] The supervisory relationship is one of those areas where a great deal of game playing goes on. Game playing is counterproductive to supervision because whenever it happens it is signaling resistance on the part of the supervisor, the supervisee or both to a significant aspect of the supervisory relationship and program. Supervisors need to be alert to the game playing process. It is easy to become frustrated about the resistance and the games when we have supervisory goals so that we do not identify the situation. When we are working under frustration rather than identifying the situation, we attempt to deal with our supervisory goals rather than the game playing but if substantial supervision is to happen, we will have to turn our attention to the game playing in order to bring it to a halt. This does not mean that supervisors will want to stop all game playing "cold turkey" because there may be some defense mechanisms which the supervisee still needs in order to function and cope. When supervisors suddenly announce that game playing is going on, they often strip the supervisees of their defensive garments and leave them naked which in turn paralyzes the supervisees so that they are unable to get on with the work of supervision. Where a student is less mature, supervisors may want to assign reading about game playing and in a routine way try to get the students to identify possible situations in which they game play. Supervisors may want to include a variety of relationships in which there may not be any apparent game playing as well as those where the game playing is obvious in order for the students to see that they are capable of relating to people straight across the board rather than a surreptitious role. There are students who are mature and understand the role of game playing so that they may be confronted precisely about the supervisor's hunches concerning their game playing. All of the game playing is not at the hands of the students because supervisors frequently get caught up in game playing. This is one reason why it is important for every supervisor to have a supervisor so that the game playing can be pointed out by a third party.

The supervisee is likely to play several games. The first of these is the supervisory split. Here students try to bring a breach between supervisors. This may be between the supervisor and the director or between the field supervisor and a supervising committee. Whenever students are successful with the supervisory split, they are able to do what they want or do nothing because the supervisors are busy checkmating one another. Clear covenants of supervision and regular communication between supervisors will help to offset the negative results of this game.

Dorothy Jongeward explains that: "Wooden leg is a cop out game played to avoid accomplishment or work. The person who plays wooden leg uses a physical or social handicap (which in itself may be real enough) as an excuse for lack of performance."[11] Students often add the psychological category to the physical and social categories. They complain that they are not as bright as another person or that they have not had a particular class or read a particular book.

Students also like to play the game "ain't it awful." In this game the students can play "ain't it awful" with their field supervisors about the school's insensitivity, lack of organization or theological stance. Whenever students play "ain't it awful" for awhile, they blunt the supervisor's sword.

Students also play "let's you and him fight." The student may make this one of the facets of the supervisory split. Students will want you and the other supervisor to fight out the solutions to problems while the student stands by and watches. Ministry students often pit supervisors over against other authorities. The student may drop a creed or the Bible in the supervisor's lap and suggest that the supervisor fight it out with the creed or the scriptures. Students may also appeal to the book of a widely respected authority and want the supervisor to fight it out with that book.

Students may also use the game of seduction. This is not the physical seduction (although it could be that) but it is the seduction by students, usually by flattery, to get supervisors to defend them, protect them, promote them or in some other way to respond favorably whether or not reality indicates that as a proper response. It is often a kind of blackmail where the supervisee says, "be nice to me because I am nice to you."

"Yes, but" is one of the most prevalent games. Here students seem to agree but show their real resistance in the end. They do not have the courage to confront directly nor are they free enough from defensiveness to hear and act on the suggestions which are made. I know of one supervisor who says that he always forgets anything that comes before "but." As long as the "yes, but" game is played, students can never get beyond themselves and their defensiveness to deal with the issues which are confronting them.

Students who play the game "kick me" seem to invite others to punish them for things which they have done. These students may go to great lengths to talk about how stupid they were or they may reveal a mistake when there was no cause to do so. These people are playing an interesting game that goes "if I tell you to kick me because of how stupid I am, you will feel as if you don't want to kick me when I am down and therefore you will begin to apologize for me and forgive me." The game "poor me" is closely related because people are putting themselves down in order to get sympathy.

The game called "harried executive" usually begins when the student takes on an ambitious load and works frantically to fulfill it. Then the frenzy becomes an excuse not to fulfill the supervisory expectations placed upon the student.

There is the game "I'll take the high road."[12] This is the game that students play when they have become educated with technical information beyond that which the people have whom they serve. Rather than meeting the life situation of the people to whom they are ministering, students become more interested in demonstrating their new found knowledge. A large part of the game playing comes when a supervisor tries to confront them because they have an answer that is a stopper: this is what they have learned in their classes or "it's the truth" and they have to stand up for it.[13]

Another insidious game is "I've done the best I can under the circumstances." Students recognize the limited results which their actions brought but justify their limited results by saying that under the circumstances they did the best they could. The implication is that there was nothing wrong with the way they functioned, that it was just the circumstances which, if changed, would mean that they would have greater results. This tends to do two things: First of all, it tends to hinder students from taking responsibility since the conditions weren't right; secondly, they do not think that a supervisor has any right to challenge them about their ministry because of the situation. They fail to realize that they are responsible regardless of the situation because there will never be any situations which are ideal for bringing about the results which they want.

In the "relevance game" students challenge academicians about the relevance of what they are saying to the "real world" out there. The students (sometimes the same students) will challenge the field supervisors about the relevance of the exercises and requirements for real academics. The game "it's all so confusing" keeps everyone off balance especially on critical issues or at critical times, by keeping everyone explaining what it is they mean or justifying what they are saying because the students claim that they cannot understand what the supervisor wants. This will be an effective game to play by students who are resisting the affective part of learning in supervision.

"I did what you told me" is a way in which the students push off onto supervisors the responsibility of what happens or what does not happen. This is especially an effective game to give difficulty to supervisors where students only halfheartedly try to carry out a behavioral change or a new approach. Whenever it goes wrong, the student is able to chop the supervisor down because the supervisor suggested the action.

Another game is "forty thousand Frenchmen can't be wrong." Whenever supervisors confront students, the students often retort that nobody else has ever told them that or that other people (supervisors, counselors or professors) have told them something else. They play a challenging game inasmuch as they challenge their supervisors to say that they are correct and the host of others who have dealt with the student have been wrong.

The game of "corner" is a way in which supervisees try to get the supervisor into an area where there is no way the supervisor can win. They may quote the supervisor's words back or point out the supervisor's own errors.

"Blemish" is a game of nitpicking over little things which of course takes the attention away from the significant areas. Players are more interested in finding somebody to be incorrect that they are dealing with supervisory issues. Supervisors can do this with student reports. They read the student reports as though they were Ph.D. theses looking for all of the commas left out or typographical errors. They make so much of these mechanical issues that substantive issues are not dealt with.

Some games are especially tempting to supervisors. One of the games is "psychiatry," in which the supervisor is always attempting to play psychiatrist with the students. They wonder what sinister situation is behind every statement and they are always looking for some kind of neurosis. There is also the game of "uproar" in which the supervisor blasts the student in a way that does not correspond to the reality which stimulated it. Whenever this uproar takes place, the emotions and the attention are drawn toward the uproar rather than toward the supervisory issue.

Many supervisors feel that game playing is part of the supervision; they purposely play a game with their supervisees to test out certain issues. No doubt supervisors have been success- ful using this method, but it can easily become counterproduc- tive. Supervisors can lose their perspective and get caught up into the game playing. Supervisors who use this method need to have adequate information about the coping mechanisms of the students or they may trigger a reaction which damage the student as well as the supervisory relationship. The best rule to follow is that one attempts to create as many authentic relationships and responses as possible.

Game playing has a good many disadvantages. Whenever a person is game playing, they do not deal with reality but with the game they have created. Because they depend so upon game playing to manipulate and get their way, they never know whether they can deal with reality or not. The longer that pattern goes, the more frightened they are of reality and become more dependent upon game playing. Patterns of game playing develop so that persons are not able to relate to people authentically but have to relate to them in a gaming fashion. One of the aspects of game playing that becomes sick is that a person who becomes so dependent upon game playing assumes that everyone else is game playing also. The result of that is that it is difficult to have authentic relationships which are straight across the board.

Alfred Kadushin says that the "supervisor-supervisee rela- tionship is evocative of the parent-child relationship and as such may tend to reactivate some anxiety associated with this earlier relationship."[14] When children learn to manipulate their parents by game playing, they continue those patterns which have been successful for them in the parent-child relationship into other relationships. If they were able to avoid responsibility in the home relationship, they will likely seek to avoid responsibility in other relationships. Where there has been great trust in the home relationship, there may even be a problem with naivete in the trust relationships that the children will have with other people in the world but if the home relationship was built on game playing, they will likely distrust others and try to manipulate others while assuming that others are trying to manipulate them.

FOOTNOTES
Chapter IV

¹Donald F. Beisswenger, "Differentiating modes of Supervision in Theological Field Education,"*Theological Education,* Vol. IX, No. 1 (Autumn, 1974). See the appendix for Beisswenger's summary chart of "Modes of Understanding the Supervisory Task."

²Alfred Kadushin, "Supervisor-Supervisee: A Survey," *Social Work,* May, 1974, p. 290.

³Ibid.

⁴Thomas W. Klink, "Supervision As a Routine Process in Professional Education for Ministry," *Duke Divinity Review,* 1968.

⁵I wish to acknowledge my debt to David A. Steere of Louisville Presbyterian Seminary for some of these categories. See David A. Steere, "An Experiment in Supervisory Training," *The Journal of Pastoral Care,* Vol. XXIII, No. 2 (December, 1969), pp. 202-217.

⁶Kathryn V. Feyereisen, A. John Fiorino and Arlene T. Nowak, *Supervision and Curriculum Renewal: A Systems Approach,* (New York: Appleton-Century-Crofts, Educational Division, Meridith Corporation, 1970), pp. 239-241.

⁷William R. Van Dersal, *The Successful Supervisor In Government and Business,* (New York, Evanston, San Francisco, London: Harper & Row Publishers, 1974), pp. 170-191.

⁸Ibid.

⁹For example, see Alan Keith-Lucas, *Giving and Taking Help,* (Chapel Hill, North Carolina: The University of North Carolina Press, 1972).

¹⁰Eric Berne, *Games People Play,* (New York: Grove Press, Inc., 1964).

¹¹Dorothy Jongeward, *Everybody Wins,* (Reading, Massachusetts: Addison-Wesley Publishing Co., 1973), p. 47.

¹²Doran C. McCarty, "Supervising Minister of Music Students," *The Southern Baptist Church Music Conference Journal,* 1978.

¹³I wish to thank Clyde Cutrer for his stimulating paper (unpublished) "Contract for Learning—Youth Music."

¹⁴Alfred Kadushin, "Games People Play in Supervision," *Journal of Social Work,* July, 1968, p. 24.

Chapter V
Evaluation in Supervision

Techniques of Evaluation

Evaluation is threatening but there is no way to escape it. Ministers may not set up committees to evaluate themselves but they are evaluated every time they preach, during the sermon, on the way home in the car and around the dinner table. Evaluation is essential for the minister's growth and for the minister to keep in touch with reality. One of my friends says that the only thing worse than finding out what somebody thinks about you is not finding out what somebody thinks about you because sooner or later you will find out when it is too late to do anything about it. Ministers usually do not get evaulation until it is too late. People will be nice to them, generally, until things reach a critical point and by then there is a breakdown in relationships because the minister has not been able to test the reality of the situation's feedback. Hopefully, within the program of supervision students can become comfortable receiving evaluation and seek it out or develop a structure to receive evaluation later in their ministry.

What Are You Evaluating?

An important question with regard to the evaluation of ministers is, "What are you evaluating?" The evaluation may be of the students acquisition of knowledge, skills, personhood or performance. Educational institutions have developed sophisticated ways to measure the acquisition of knowledge but they have few ways of evaluating skills, personhood and performance. Since students have been in school for a good many years, most of them have learned how to function during evaluations of their acquisition of knowledge by tests, but they are likely to be frustrated by any kind of attempt to evaluate their skills, personhood or performance. Some will even be highly resistant. The evaluation in the supervised ministry should be of the student's performance, especially performing through ministry. Certainly the examination of performance leads back to problems in the acquisition of knowledge, skills and personhood and the student may have to deal with these when the evaluation of their performance indicates that there is a problem in one or more of these areas.

The criteria for evaluation should be set out at the beginning clearly so that there are no negative surprises when the evaluation comes. The basic instrument for setting forth the criteria for evaluation will be the covenant of learning. The covenant of learning will spell out the expectations the school and supervisor have of the student. When the period of evaluation comes, supervisors may have found other issues which they believe should be dealt with but they are limited to the terms of the covenant of learning. If it is going to be inadequate, they need to re-negotiate it with mutuality but until that is done the original covenant stands as the criteria for evaluation.

What is the Goal of Evaluation?

There are several possible goals for evaluation. The evaluation may be used for judgment. This is where the student is brought into the supervisor's tribunal for the judgment to be passed upon the students as to whether they performed satisfactorily or not. Another goal of evaluation may be learning. This is a legitimate goal of evaluation because as the students get feedback they ought to be able to use that information and integrate it in their learning process. Rather than evaluation being the deadend street of judgment, it should be opening up new avenues of learning for the student. In this way the evaluation process becomes an agenda-building process. When students go through evaluation, they should have their agenda for the next few months sharpened and perhaps even new agenda added that they will be working on in the next several months. While it will never be stated, there are times when the goal of evaluation is for the supervisor to parade his authority much like a peacock parades his tail feathers. This is not only a travesty of supervision but it can be very harmful to the students.

What Will the Evaluation Be Used For?

The real, legitimate reason for evaluation is for the profit of students, both by giving feedback about their performance and giving the supervisor an opportunity to check out some things with the students. In many situations evaluation will also be used for grading the student or to determine whether a student will pass or fail a course. Whenever that is the case, an entirely new set of dynamics is introduced. The evaluation may even be so expansive as to be necessary for the student to receive a good evaluation in order to graduate. In some cases evaluations are used for placement purposes. This probably obstructs the process of evaluation more than anything else. Where evaluation is used for something other than the learning process itself, there will be resistance, game playing and little openness. While it is necessary for every institution to decide upon the use of evaluation, school administrators should look seriously at the possibility that non-learning uses of evaluation can thwart the first and foremost goal of evaluation and field education programs. Whatever the use of supervision, the school must have a clear contract with a student at the beginning about what use will be made of the evaluations.

Who Is Able to Evaluate?

Supervisors are in a unique position to evaluate students. In fact that is a serious and major part of the responsibility of supervisors. They are with the students, receive their work reports and have supervisory sessions with them which gives them the data for evaluation. Supervisees themselves are also able to evaluate. They are able to check some things out about themselves. They know some of their inner feelings as no one else can know them. Student peers are able to evaluate. There are things which students can hide from supervisors which they cannot hide from their peers. There is understanding which flows back and forth among students which a supervisor can never be a party to. Laypersons can also evaluate. They have a perspective which no one else has and they are the real and final audience (judges) of the students.

When Should Evaluation Take Place?

The evaluation happens the first time that we see someone. We will think that they are bright or dull, ambitious or lazy, kind or hateful. This is not the way evaluation ought to be done but it is the way that it is done. This makes it important for supervisors to structure their evaluation to make sure they avoid all the pitfalls that are possible. Evaluation should take place throughout the supervisory relationship. Every week when the supervisor and supervisee meet together, the supervisor should give some indication to the students how they are fulfilling the supervisor's expectations. There should be a formal evaluation at the mid-point in the supervisory relationship. This is a mid-point correction possibility so that the student can begin to move in a different direction. The supervisor has had long enough to check a few hunches out in order not to overreact. The mid-point evaluation should be to give feedback to the students and to ask them to test out certain hypotheses which the supervisor has about the students. There should also be a highly structured final evaluation where the supervisor sums up the whole relationship and asks the student to help in the summation.

Group and Individual Evaluation

There are advocates of group and individual supervision and both have advantages. However, when it comes to evaluation, group supervision has some special advantages. Supervisors are not just dependent upon their own insights but have the insights of others in the group. This makes the evaluation a much safer and better balanced evaluation. Group evaluation can also use the advantage of individual evaluations as well. It is especially helpful to many students for the supervisor to hold individual evaluation sessions following group evaluations. Sometimes there are wounds which the group inflicts upon the student which the supervisor can either bind up or at least clean out so that they won't get infected.

How a Supervisor Goes About Evaluation

Directors and supervisors feel a panic brought on by the word "evaluation." They begin to seek for evaluation forms which will be adequate to "judge" the students. Of course there are instruments which are helpful in the evaluation process but none of them do the job adequately because you cannot get the true picture of a person on a true-false quiz the way that you can discover whether a student has read a book by giving a true-false quiz. There are also too many different kinds of ministry settings for one evaluation form to deal adequately with the progress of all students. Directors have devised many different evaluation forms. Below is a form which Dr. G. Willis Bennett used at Southern Baptist Theological Seminary.

Southern Baptist Theological Seminary
Field Education Evaluation
Non-Pastor Placements

Student_____ Conference group _____

Church or agency_____ Student position_____

Supervisor _____ Period of evaluation_____

Date student began this position _____

    I. Describe the responsibilities assigned to this student this semester:

Please rank this student by circling the number representative of your honest evaluation of his/her performance this semester. 5=Superior, 4=Excellent, 3=Acceptable, 2=Fair, 1=Unsatisfactory, 0=Not Applicable.

    II. **Personal work habits**

Punctuality	5	4	3	2	1	0
Keeping appointments	5	4	3	2	1	0
Handles absences responsibly	5	4	3	2	1	0
Preparation for assignments	5	4	3	2	1	0
Personal appearance	5	4	3	2	1	0
Flexibility	5	4	3	2	1	0
Goes beyond minimal requirements	5	4	3	2	1	0

    Remarks:

III. **Relation to church or agency**

Accepts limits of setting	5	4	3	2	1	0
Meets agency obligations	5	4	3	2	1	0
Understands agency goals and objectives	5	4	3	2	1	0
Committed to its goals and objectives	5	4	3	2	1	0
Follows proper channels in functioning	5	4	3	2	1	0

Remarks:

IV. **Relationships with people**

Able to relate with warmth and interest	5	4	3	2	1	0
Works comfortably with staff	5	4	3	2	1	0
Relates to individuals on a one-to-one basis	5	4	3	2	1	0
Relates to individuals as a group	5	4	3	2	1	0
Relates to groups as a whole	5	4	3	2	1	0
Relates well to community people	5	4	3	2	1	0
Honest in feelings toward others	5	4	3	2	1	0
Assumes responsibility for his or her part in relationships	5	4	3	2	1	0

Remarks:

V. **Functioning within expected role**

Exercises initiative in fulfilling assignments	5	4	3	2	1	0
Protects confidentiality	5	4	3	2	1	0
Demonstrates ability to integrate classroom theory with field assignment	5	4	3	2	1	0
Aware of community resources	5	4	3	2	1	0
Utilizes community resources	5	4	3	2	1	0
Understands role as helping (enabling) individuals	5	4	3	2	1	0
Understands program as a part of Christian ministry	5	4	3	2	1	0
Is creative in completion of tasks	5	4	3	2	1	0
Is a good leader	5	4	3	2	1	0

Remarks:

VI. **Supervisory relationship**

Understands the process of supervision	5	4	3	2	1	0
Assumes responsibility for participation in conference	5	4	3	2	1	0
Submits records when required	5	4	3	2	1	0

Handles well criticism directed to-
ward him   5   4   3   2   1   0
Evaluates supervisor's suggestions
before acting upon them   5   4   3   2   1   0
How often have you met with student?

Remarks:

VII. Recommended changes in field education assignment next
semester?

VIII. Recommended education goals for next semester?

IX. Suggested grade (circle one)
A+   A   A−   B+   B   B−   C+   C   C−   D+   D   D−   F

Signed _____

Position _____

Date _____

Signature of
(I have reviewed this form.)   student _____

Date _____

(Please return as soon as possible to G. Willis Bennett, director of field
education, Southern Baptist Theological Seminary, 2825 Lexington
Road, Louisville, Kentucky 40206.)

Another avenue of evaluation is for the supervisors to keep a
supervisory log. This gives some evaluation material to the
students every month when the supervisor prepares the log to
send to the director. Students begin to see in bite sizes the issues
which the supervisor raises about their work. Below is the sample
of a weekly log which Masters level supervisors are requested to
fill out each week to hand in at the monthly supervisors meeting.
Inasmuch as the students have to sign the report, students can
see how they are being perceived as they go along instead of it
being one great surprise at the end.

Week Number		Supervisor	Date

Supervisory Period		Student	Date

FIELD SUPERVISOR'S LOG

1. Contacts with supervisee:
2. Supervisory meetings (when, where, how long):
3. Work submitted by student:
4. Subjects initiated by student:
5. Subjects initiated by supervisor:
6. Issues of supervision:
7. Assignments:
8. Ongoing concerns:
9. Recommendations:

The narrative report is the most indepth and productive kind of evaluation. This report is where the supervisor writes out in narrative fashion answers to questions about work, relationships and meaningfulness relative to the program of the student. These narrative evaluation forms give the supervisors opportunities to report adequately on the kind of ministry which the student is doing regardless of the type of ministry setting. There is an opportunity on each point to give both the positive and the negative patterns of the supervisees. They are also able to illustrate why they have made the evaluation which they have written. Below is a copy of an evaluation form which is used to help guide supervisors in writing up a narrative report.

GUIDELINES FOR SUPERVISOR'S SIX-MONTH EVALUATION OF D. MIN. CANDIDATES

The supervisor will want to develop his/her evaluation of each candidate. He/she will give one copy to the candidate and one to the director.

* 1. OVERVIEW

    The supervisor will relate the basic supervisory structure during the past six months and offer general impressions as to how "things have gone."

* 2. EVALUATION OF CANDIDATE'S D. MIN. WORK

    The supervisor will evaluate the work produced for the D. Min. program during the past six months and its significance and learning value.

* 3. EVALUATION OF WORK DONE BY CANDIDATE IN MINISTRY SETTING

The supervisor will evaluate the candidate's work level in his/her ministry setting, the meaningfulness of that work and the candidate's effectiveness.

* 4. CANDIDATE'S RELATIONSHIPS WITH THOSE IN THE PEER GROUP

The supervisor will evaluate the candidate's relationship with each member of the peer group referring to specific incidents which illustrate.

* 5. CANDIDATE'S RELATIONSHIPS WITH PEOPLE IN MINISTRY SETTING

The supervisor will give general impressions as to how the candidate relates to people in his/her ministry setting and any changes taking place. Please illustrate with anecdotes.

* 6. CANDIDATE'S RELATIONSHIP WITH SUPERVISOR

The supervisor will give impressions about the formal and informal relationships between supervisor and supervisee giving accounts of incidents which illustrate.

* 7. CANDIDATE'S ABILITY TO INTEGRATE CONCEPTUAL INTO FUNCTIONING

The candidate should give evidence of being able to take the conceptualizations from previous learning experiences and the D. Min. seminars and function appropriate to those conceptualizations. Please relate incidents which illustrate your evaluations. This should include his/her ability to see the theological significance of what is happening and therefore his/her ability to theologize.

* 8. EVALUATION OF CANDIDATE'S MINISTRY IDENTITY

Evaluate the candidate's perception of his/her role identity as a minister and his/her ability to fulfill that role with integrity. Please relate incidents to illustrate.

* 9. EVALUATION OF CANDIDATE'S PERSONAL IDENTITY

Evaluate the candidate's perception of who he or she is as well as his/her ego strength, perception of sexual roles, personality integration and his/her understanding of the dynamics involved in these. Please give incidents to illustrate.

*10. EVALUATION OF CANDIDATE'S ABILITY TO DEAL WITH STRESS
Please relate incidents to illustrate.

*11. EVALUATION OF CANDIDATE'S ABILITY TO DEAL WITH STRUCTURES

Evaluate the candidate's perceptions of formal and informal structures and his/her ability to handle these and be a change agent with them. Also include how the candidate is able to function where he/she faces non-structured situations or where he/she is placed in an unfamiliar structure. Please relate incidents that illustrate.

*12. EVALUATION OF CANDIDATE'S ABILITY TO INITIATE

Evaluate the candidate's ability to take leadership in structured situations and in situations that need to be structured. Please relate incidents that illustrate.

*13. RELATE YOUR GOALS WITH THIS CANDIDATE DURING THE NEXT SIX MONTHS (UNLESS THIS IS THE FINAL EVALUATION)

These goals shoud be related to his/her contract for learning. However, these goals shoud also be set in response to problem areas of the candidate's work, functioning or personhood.

*Please relate incidents which illustrate your evaluation. If it is only a "feeling" and you have no illustrations, please relate that.

When supervisors hold evaluation sessions with the students, they need to request students to prepare written evaluations drawn up on the lines consistent with what is required in the program. In group supervision students should read their evaluations aloud after which all the other persons in the group can respond to the evaluation. If it is individual supervision, then the dialogue should begin between the supervisor and the student. The evaluation session needs to get at the questions: "How is the supervisee doing?" "How is the relationship going between the supervisor and supervisee?" "What needs to be done next?" Beyond these questions supervisors need to state specifically how they see the students doing. Are the students meeting the criteria set out in the covenant of learning? Are they merely going through the motions to fulfill the covenant of learning or are they attempting to accomplish something? The supervisors also should give the students feedback on how the supervisory relationship is going and what are the areas that need to be worked on there.

Grid Evaluation

Grid evaluation is where the director (or supervisor) takes a great deal of material which has been amassed about this student and puts it altogether and tries to draw a profile from all of the data for the student. It is a grid system much like rock quarries passing rocks through different size mesh in order to screen out the various sizes of rock. The supervisee's experiences are put through the grid in order to see the patterns which appear in the different experiences or the reactions which appear differently in one set of experiences than another. This grid system may include information about preaching, personality, inventories, lay evaluation, self-evaluation, peer evaluation, supervisory evaluation, ministry logs and ministry contacts. There is an element of safety in grid evaluations inasmuch as the data comes from several different sources and it does not run the risk of being only one person's (the supervisor's) opinion about the students.

Issues in Evaluation

Whatever the form of the evaluation process, it is the content which counts. The content of the evaluation is made up of issues which all people have to deal with, especially ministers and more particularly students.

Several issues are dealt with in evaluation: conceptual knowledge, skills and personhood (affective).

When evaluating conceptual knowledge, it is important to be able to determine how much data students have been able to become exposed to and retain. However, a lot of "walking encyclopedias" have never been able to find the meaning of the data which they have. Ministry students must become selective in their data on the basis of its meaningfulness. Emphasis should be made with the ministry student on the ability of the student to integrate this conceptual data with functioning in ministry. Each person can list areas in which the ministry student should have conceptual knowledge: biblical, theological, language, psychological, sociological, etc.

Supervisors will need to evaluate student's ministry skills. Students need to gain skills in all of the areas appropriate for their ministry. Inasmuch as supervisors will often be dealing with students who are somewhat immature, the supervisors should be aware that immature students are likely to be fadish or exclusively enthralled by one particular kind of ministry. The students may be so exclusively given to evangelism, counseling or social activism that they fail to develop the wider range of skills that they will need in their later ministry when they will have to touch all the bases. The supervisor will be able to make a list of the kinds of ministry skills which will be needed such as preaching, teaching, administrating, performing the rites of baptism, the Lord's supper and marriage and other functions needed in ministry roles. However, it is not only the number of skills which will be needed but also the level at which these skills should be developed. There will certainly be a difference in expectation between the level of skills of freshmen college students and graduate students in a seminary so that the level of skill development needs to be set out. One of the important aspects of the covenant of learning is to set out the level of skills as clearly as possible. There are some objective ways to get at the evaluation of some skills but ultimately the test is how one person comes across to another person in bringing about the desired ministry.

The third area of issues for evaluation is that of the personhood of a student related to the affective approach to learning. This area is far more threatening to the supervisor and the supervisee because they are more nebulous and because they are closer to where a person really lives. Often it is very difficult to get handles on this area because we sense there is something there but we are not able to name it. Once we are able to name it, we will be able to deal with it. I find that supervisors are very concerned about how to get started and how to get at this part of supervision. Because of that difficulty, I am giving a list of possible issues to examine with supervisees. These issues form something of a grid the supervisor can use. During a time when a supervisor is trying to sort out things about the supervisee, the supervisor can mentally put the student through these various grids in order to determine what the supervisor's opinion is about the student in each one of these areas. Hopefully when supervisors have completed this exercise, they will be able to develop a portrait of the student to present to the student to try on for reality and to stimulate the student to use the evaluation for new learning experiences. The personhood area of supervision is related basically to personal relationships with people. These 38 different areas listed below represents a refraction which happens when human experiences are put through the prism of supervision.

1. *Work*

Supervisors need to question their student's capacity for work; different people have different energy levels. Specifically the supervisors should examine the work level which has been followed during the course of the student's field ministry. Students may be able to function with a great deal of energy in the classroom but find that they are blocking so badly in field ministry that they have to use an inordinate amount of energy in order to function.

It is also important to examine the meaningfulness of the work which the students do. Students may find work to be very meaningless and therefore do not expend much energy in work but on the other hand there may be some workoholics who are neurotically driven to work because they never get enough meaning out of their work to satisfy them. They try to make up in quantity for the quality which is missing in work for them. The meaningfulness also extends to the kind of work that they do. Some students will find that the only work that is meaningful to them is work that is dramatic or grandiose; they do not find any meaningfulness in the routine aspects of ministry. These students will usually only find meaningfulness in the work which is their agenda and meets their needs rather than work which meets the needs of other people. It is interesting, however, when students find unusual meaningfulness in routine, housekeeping type of work. These will be dependent people who are afraid to risk so they stay with the safe, routine, pedantic chores. How the students are able to sustain a work level, especially without outside stimuli, will be a helpful indicator of the student's mark of maturity.

2. *Authority*

Supervisors will want to take note how their students handle authority. Do they become rebellious against authority or adaptive to authority figures? What are the reactions of the students in the presence of authority figures? Do the students avoid authority or do they seek authority figures out even when the situation does not demand or suggest it? Do the students have a sense of their own authority and do they claim it? Ministers use authority which is official, from their calling or from their personhood. Do the students under supervision try to get things done through their own personal authority rather than their calling as a minister or do the students rely upon official authority rather than taking initiative to exert their authority?

3. *Initiating*

Initiating describes the student's ability to take the lead to solve problems and develop relationships. Whenever students are overly dependent, they cannot initiate properly. Some students are able to initiate when there is a strong structure that they understand and work within while other students are able to initiate where there is an absence of structure or even where there is resistance. Some students are able to initiate with regard to organizational matters while others are able to initiate relationships but have difficulty in projecting initiation with organizations. Initiating is an important aspect of the student's learning process because the ability to take initiative overcomes many of the problems. Students who are passive and wait for things to happen cannot exercise their gifts as positively. There are problems when students are compulsive and have to be the ones who always take initiative but supervisors can probably more easily harness and check such manic initiators than they can recharge passive persons and help them develop the courage to risk initiation.

4. *Sex roles*

Students need to become aware of and comfortable with their appropriate sex roles and how they relate to others and their perceived or actual sex roles. During the period in which students are moving from adolescence to adulthood, sex roles become acutely important. However, the American society is now in turmoil over sex roles and ministry students cannot escape this turmoil. It will be important to notice whether the student feels more comfortable working with women or working with men. It will also be important to see how the students use the sex role issue prevalent in our American society in relationship to their work as a student and as a minister. While it may be common for some students to avoid dealing with the sex role issue, there are students caught up in the sexual revolution and expend their energies in the liberation movement while at the same time avoiding other important supervisory issues.

5. *Theologizing*

Theologizing is starting with experience and finding the theological themes inherent in and appropriate to that experience. Every action has theological ramifications although some are more clearly apparent and others more complex. Theologizing is the attempt to help students to integrate their theological and biblical knowledge by being able to apply them to the experiences which they face. Theologizing also examines the student's confessed theology and the theological presuppositions inherent in the student's actions in order to see whether or not these are consistent with one another. If they are not consistent, the students should attempt to change their actions in the light of their confessed theology or re-examine their confessed theology to see if it is adequate. At times, students have to claim the hiatus between their confessed theology and their actions and hold the two in tension until they are able to resolve the paradox.

6. *Investments*

People have emotional and personal investments in causes, ideas or memories. These investments may have been expressed by monetary means, time given or emotional identification. Supervisors need to find out how their students are conscious of these investments and appreciate the investments of other people as well as seeing if the students are aware of their own investments.

7. *Power structures*

Students need to learn to recognize formal and informal power structures and the powers inherent in them. They need to know the dangers inherent in working with these power structures and their ability to be a change agent while working with these power structures. They need to learn to accept and use appropriately the power that they have or receive. The minister has three sources of power: official, call and personal.[1] Students may refuse to move except where they have been empowered by official action of the group. Others may try to solve all problems on a personal basis (either friendship or charm) rather than on the basis of who they are.

8. *Personal structure*

Students will need to find the importance of structure for them as ministers. Their lives need to be structured in relationship to their use of time and groups. They need to be aware of their need of that structure, when they use it, when they depend on it and when it gets in the way or relating to people or functioning within organizations.

9. *Agendas*

Student ministers must learn the importance of having their own agenda and becoming conscious that they have an agenda. They also must become aware of the agenda of other persons they encounter. They need the ability to read the agendas of people whether or not others are able to own their own agenda.

10. *Contracts*

"Contract" is a metaphorical expression for discovering the content of relationships based on the expectations which people bring to those relationships. This includes formal, informal and tacit contracts. Students need to be able to learn what contracts are made and how they must be kept and how to raise to consciousness the contracts which are never really spelled out. They need to know the contracts which situations automatically impose upon people.

11. *Conflict*

Supervisors should examine how students function in conflict situations. They need to see if the students are able to identify the elements of conflict and develop methods for dealing with it creatively. Also the supervisor should see how the students handle the anger that conflict creates within themselves and other persons.

12. *Transitions*

Students need to give pastoral care to persons in transitions. Supervisors should evaluate that and how much the students are aware of what happens in the multi-occurring transitions. How much are the students able to use rites to facilitate these life transitions? Students also undergo transitions so that the supervisor will be able to examine how the students handle change themselves. These changes may be intellectual as they face new theological ideas and challenges or they may be personal as they marry or have children come into the family or as they move from the role of student to minister.

13. *Loss*

Students should be aware of the dimensions and types of losses which occur in human experience. The supervisor needs to examine how the students are sensitive to and minister in these kinds of experiences. Students also may have losses through accident, health situations, the loss of family members or romantic losses. Supervisors should not only help students through these loss situations, but help them to identify what is going on and make them learning experiences.

14. *Discipline*

The supervisor will want to examine how much the students are getting in charge of their time, schedule, energy and ministry resources. This will mean the development of intentional regimentation on the part of the student.

15. *Anxiety*

Supervisors need to examine the nature and make-up of systems of anxiety both in extreme cases and in the student's everyday experience. This becomes very important in the supervisory process because anxiety may block the student's ability to function. However, it may be even more serious than that because the symptoms of anxiety may indicate a serious problem which needs to be dealt with before the student experiences serious trauma or even a psychological breakdown.

16. *Self-identity*

Students need to develop a self-identity because they are usually moving from adolescence to adulthood which causes fluctuation in their perception of their self-identity. The students are being pushed into many different roles by such diverse persons as parents, professors, peers and society.

17. *Ministry identity*

Students need to be able to integrate their self-identity into a ministry identity. They will tend to subjugate one identity to the other. Some will deny their personal identity to take upon themselves a ministry identity while others will try to be "authentic" human beings and they will see that as having to shy away from a ministry identity. These students will be uncomfortable in a ministry identity and role. There will be others who will be able to take on a ministry identity and role and use it remaining conscious of their real self-identity.

18. *Affirmation*

Supervisors need to see where students get their affirmation and whether or not they are able to accept healthy affirmation. The students also need to learn to "bless" and affirm others.

19. *Resistance*

As supervisors meet resistance in students, they should determine the source and cause of that resistance and whether that resistance is a response to reality or not. They should look for the patterns in the students' resistance as to whether they resist people or ideas and what kinds of people or ideas they resist.

20. *Defenses*

The supervisors should find out what defense mechanisms the students have, how they use them and whether they still need them or not. If they do not need them, the supervisor will note that they can eliminate them. If they do need them, the supervisor should note whether the students use them in such a way to minimize their negative effect or if they are effectively blocking the students' functioning.

21. *Personal strengths*

The supervisor should assess whether or not the students are able to identify and own their personal strengths. The supervisor will need to ascertain whether the students are able or willing to use the personal strengths which they have.

22. *Definition of issues*

The supervisor needs to ask how well the students can define issues in given situations. The students should be able to articulate the issues in language that is appropriate to the nature of the issues as well as in "God language" and theological verbalization.

23. *Ability to focus*

Supervisors will want to examine the ability of students to focus their attention and efforts on issues which need attention without the diffusion of their energies which hinders them from bringing their powers to bear significantly upon areas of life and ministry.

24. Functioning in non-structured role situations

Students will not only function in areas where there is a structured role (preaching, classroom teaching, etc.) but also in areas where the role is not structured. Supervisors need to find out whether students can initiate in non-structured role situations the same as they function in structured role situations.

25. Functioning at different levels

The supervisor should test out the students abilities to function at different levels. This will include functioning with people at different religious, intellectual and social levels. They also need to function with non-clergy as well as clergy and in non-religious scenarios as well as religious structures. They should also determine the students' ability to function in various levels of intimacy.

26. Religious language

Supervisors need to be aware of the students' investment and use of religious language. The students may be overly dependent upon religious language or they may use religious language to cover up areas which need to be clarified and dealt with. They may use religious language to avoid being pressed on issues. On the other hand students may avoid religious language because they are uncomfortable in a ministry role or they may not feel comfortable with or accept people who do use religious language.

27. Intellectualizing

Supervisors need to evaluate the students' intellectualizing to determine their tendency to theorize about situations rather than doing something about them. Some students feel comfortable and that they have done all there is to be done when they have explained why situations have happened rather than ministering to the situations.

28. Spiritualizing

Students sometimes interpret all experiences in "God language" and by offering divine or demonic answers to all of human experience. Supervisors will need to evaluate these tendencies and see how well the students are in touch with reality as they do this.

29. Spiritual formation

Supervisors can help by evaluating the development of the discipline of a personal devotional life in the students and helping them to integrate it with the vocational life which they follow. This may require a religious history in order to find out how the students have developed step by step in the process.

30. *Perception of reality*
Supervisors need to give special care to how students perceive reality and act on the basis of reality rather than fantasy or wish. Students can distort reality because of their presuppositions, naivete and immature judgment.

31. *Internalized direction*
Supervisors should examine whether the students have internalized their sense of direction or whether their sense of direction comes from archaic parent tapes or from external pressures and forces. They should also take into account whether the students are too dependent upon the supervisor or other school structures because the time will come when they will not have a supervisor or the structures to determine their course of action.

32. *The ability to risk*
This relates to the students' ability to move into areas where the outcome is uncertain for ministry, the institution or the person. Here the supervisor examines the students' willingness or unwillingness to become vulnerable. The students' ability to move with intentionality and initiative will show up in their ability to risk. The examination of risking will probably also show what is significant enough to the students that they are afraid to risk.

33. *Response to failure*
Supervisors will become aware of the students' responses to failures. They may develop patterns in their responses to failure including setting themselves up to failure. Also there are students who go through a cycle from failure to anger to depression and they need to be in touch with that cycle. There also is the rare student who seemingly never fails and will face some serious difficulties if or when they once do fail.

34. *Revealing of self*
The supervisor will have some sense about how much the students are able to reveal themselves. This should also be looked upon as how appropriate it is. The students may want to "spill" themselves inappropriately to people they hardly know or those persons who can utilize such information to hurt them. There are others who become so rigid that they are unable to reveal anything about themselves that is significant.

35. *Awareness of contexts of ministry*

Supervisors can observe students to discover whether the students are aware of the contexts of their ministry because they will never minister in a vacuum. The supervisor will want to ask if the student sees the contexts of family, congregation, the larger community of faith, the secular community and the confessional group of which the student is a member.

36. *Awareness of the publics of the students' ministry*

Students are not always aware of who the publics are to whom they should address their ministry. Their publics can usually be named as the congregation, the community and the confessional group to which they belong.

37. *Integrate theory and practice*

Students are students in the classroom as well as the field of ministry and it is important for them to be able to integrate these two circles of influence. They need to learn to practice this early so that they will not move through their ministry wondering about what their education is all about but putting theory into practice and understanding practice in light of the theory in which they learn.

38. *Personal relating*

Here the supervisors will examine the students' ability to relate to other persons and what those patterns of relating are. Are they abrasive, flattering, loving or hateful? Do they relate to people as parent, adult or child?

This is not an exhaustive list. Supervisors may want to develop a list in language which would be more in keeping with their style of supervision.

FOOTNOTES
Chapter V

¹I wish to thank my friend, Ernie White, for pointing these out. White is pastor of the Wyatt Park Baptist Church, St. Joseph, Missouri, and has supervised students in the Midwestern Baptist Theological Seminary doctoral program since its beginning.

Chapter VI
Students Using Supervision for Learning Ministry

The Student's Role in Supervision

The student's role in supervision is primarily that of a team member along with the supervisor, the director, peers and members of the congregation (or other setting). This is in keeping with Joe Gross' analogy of supervision as being like the old two-man railroad pushcart where each pushes the handle in order to create momentum which carries the cart down the track. Supervision is a team effort with the student's role as a team member as absolutely necessary and where the student fails to carry the load of a team member, supervision will break down or be impeded. George Hunter says: "In professional education at a graduate level if a *student is not in charge of his/her own learning,* then the educational experiences will prove inadequate."[1] Hunter quotes Donald S. Amussen, chaplain at Massachusetts General Hospital in Boston:

> . . . we consider the student to be the captain of his learning team. He is supervised and there is a mutually agreed upon contract which is open for review, revision, and reconsideration during supervisory conferences. But we consider the student to be in charge of his learning. We may, and indeed do, assist him, confront him, support him, question him about his work; but what he learns and how well he learns is up to him.[2]

Ultimately the responsibility for supervision belongs to the student. While Hunter has referred to graduate level students, the same is true with college students even if the supervisors must take more initiative and the supervisory structure must be more rigid.

The students' role in supervision is a dynamic role rather than a static one. Students begin with a need to learn the structure and what the expectations are, but move from that to where they become more in charge of the activities and setting the structure of supervision. Supervisors and students should not be concerned only with whether or not the student is learning but also be concerned whether the students are at the place that they should be at each point in the supervisory program.

The role of students in supervision is the role of the learner. While supervisors, directors and professors are not perfect, the purpose of supervision is to bring about change in *students.* The role of a learner is not one of a passive person but of a person actively engaged in the process of seeking and learning. Students may be tempted to be ministers rather than learners during their supervisory process. While it is true that they should exercise both gifts, their primary role is that of being a learner for the sake of being more effective ministers in the future.

The role of students in supervision is that of being ministers in training. They do not have the full responsibility and role of being ministers, yet at the same time they are doing ministry. Being ministers in training, they are not under the full responsibility of the ministry situation in which they are taking their training; the field supervisor bears that responsibility. Students under supervision are not ministers on trial but ministers in training. They are not ministers in psycho-therapy, but ministers in training.

Another role of the students in supervision is that they are seekers. While they are seekers of knowledge, they are seeking more than knowledge. They are seeking a life vocation and through their supervised training they are able to put on that vocation and test it out in order to see whether the experience confirms the call which they have professed. They are not only seekers of truth but they are seekers of who they are and who they should be. Because supervision is dynamic, it is important that supervised students are seekers. The role of students under supervision is not to wait passively to see what comes about but to be actively seeking personal identity and to bring things about.

Self-discipline is an important role for the students in supervision. The classroom for supervision is not the four walls inside of a building but the world and specifically the ministry setting. Where the students are confined within the four walls, others can supply a strong measure of discipline to see that disciplined and professional procedures are followed to bring about the desired results. Field supervision cannot provide the same kind of tight discipline so students must supply self-discipline. Whereas the professor in the classroom has an important role to play to provide specific discipline, the field supervisor cannot provide that same type of discipline. Therefore, one of the necessary roles of students is to supply self-discipline.

If supervision is to be successful, students must take upon themselves the role of self-disclosure. While there are instruments which will help the supervisors know what is going on with the students, the only way in which supervision can take place is when the student is willing to open himself up to others. Self-disclosure on the part of the student is as important as the supervisor's role of evaluation and feedback because where there is no self-disclosure there are very limited possibilities for evaluation and feedback. The students' role in a classroom situation is to read the books and know the answers, but the students' role in supervisor situations is to do ministry and disclose what happened in the ministry and what happened to them. This self-disclosure includes the disclosure of what one intended, what one did, what one thought, what one felt and the evaluation of all of this.

Students also have the role of self-evaluators. The supervisor is not someone divine who has supernatural powers to tell students who they are and what they should do but they are persons who can evaluate and give feedback so that students will have additional input in order to do self-evaluation. All of the supervisor's evaluations are preliminary and tentative; it is the evaluations by the students themselves which are final and definitive. Students need to take the input from the supervisors and make evaluations about themselves and what they should or should not do. Students need to integrate and synthesize the intellectual data which they get with what they experience and the feedback which they receive from their supervisors. The student's job is not to lay one stone of data upon another stone of data but to shape the stones as building blocks to create a minister in the ministry.

Integrating Theory and Practice

Academic institutions compartmentalize learning. This can be seen by the way educational institutions breakdown into divisions and departments and make curriculum requirements by divisions and departments. Beyond this compartmentalization is the dichotomy in educational institutions between the academic material in the classroom and the functioning in life and vocation. One role of the student is to integrate the theory of the classroom and the practice of the vocation in life.

There is worthwhileness in theory and propriety in practice. The theory sets forth the base and the meaningfulness. Without the theory, students would not understand what is happening around them and even worse, they may drift letting expedient things happen rather than intentionally determining what happens on the basis of the appropriate theory about what ought to happen. Nothing takes the place of cognitive and conceptual knowledge. Conceptualization is the form and the base from which all activity will take place and the infrastructure upon which all practice will be built. In the same way there is propriety in practice. There may be a legitimate reason to talk about art for art's sake and knowledge for knowledge's sake, but in the ministry knowledge not only has value in and of itself but it has utilitarian value. Ministers are to practice their ministry. The student of the classroom and supervision should refuse to practice "the right hand not knowing what the left hand does." There is a temptation among students to identify with their classroom professors and develop a "despisement" of the practice of ministry as non-academic. There are also students who are action-oriented and want to "get out doing" and do not see value in learning about the conceptualizations and norms of ministry.

The role of the student, therefore, is to be an integrator and a synthesizer of conceptualizations and practice in their ministry. This is a role which, in the final analysis, only the student can fulfill. The classroom professor does not have the student's field experience and the field supervisor is not in the classroom. It is students who have gained the input of the professors and have had their unique experiences so it is up to them to integrate these.

Bill Yolton and Ron Gariboldi led the workshop on "The Integration of Theology and Experience." In this workshop they gave a model for integration. The four steps in the model were:

a. *Confrontation* by the experience;
b. *Diagnosis:* utilizing the tools of the social scientist as aides to understanding and articulating the issues;
c. *Correlation:* the issues seen in the light of theological understandings;
d. *Response:* performing ministerial acts informed by the reflection.[3]

The students get a double image on a screen made up of the academic and practical so that within themselves the students need to bring the two images together where they make one single integrated image.

Theologizing

Students need to learn more than theological words and functions; they need to learn to theologize. James and Evelyn Eaton Whitehead define theological reflection as: ". . . critical correlation of experience and Christian Tradition."[4] Francis O'Hare, formerly of St. John's Theological Seminary, Brighton, Massachusetts, defined theological reflection as:

. . . the process of looking back (i.e., thinking and feeling) on supervised pastoral experiences (either group or singly) in order to learn and grow in the appreciation of God's mysterious presence and inner action with man as man (i.e., the individual in relationship to himself, society, people of God, church).[5]

It is interesting how many educational institutions have

produced ministers who are able to look at experiences with people and see what is happening to them psychologically and to look at communities and to see what is happening to them sociologically, but have a very difficult time seeing the theological implications in the experiences which are going on around them. Theologizing is important for the students to begin to see because it means that the students can see where God is at work in their midst.

Several people have developed methods of theologizing or theological reflection.[6] Most of these methods have several aspects in common and most of these characteristics will be included in the process which I will describe below.

The first element in theologizing is a ministry experience. There are times when some of life's experiences become meaningful exercises for theologizing even though the person was not in a particular act of ministry when it happened. You need to find out the facts about the experience, including its history, the dynamics in it, the persons involved as well as the interior and exterior conditions. This stage demands a purely descriptive attempt to recapture the moment as nearly as possible. It is not necessary to deliver the experience in a neat, symmetrical way.

The second step in theologizing is the theological correlation. This is the point at which you need to discover the meaningfulness of the event. You need to discover the theological issues which were operative in the experience. You will want to relate appropriate biblical material and seek a biblical parallel to the experience. Then you can begin to find theologians who dealt forcefully with the theological issue or issues which you have uncovered. You may be at the point at which you can name the experience thus symbolizing what was the theological heart of the issue.

The third step in theologizing is finding the contemporary theological meaning in the experience which is being put through the theological prism. You are wanting to find out how God is at work in this particular situation. What is the pattern and the meaning of the presence and power of God in the experience which is being examined? God's mystery means that He is always hidden at the same time that he is being revealed, so how is it that God is revealed amidst the hiddenness of the experience which is being examined?

The last step in the theologizing process is ministry initiative. On the basis of the experience, the discovered theological issues and the power and the presence of God in the experience, what decisions need to be made to make this situation the most fruitful experience and the most in keeping with what God is trying to do in the situation? The process comes to the end of the cycle with a degree of intentionality based upon one's experience, God's truths and God's relevance.

Students in supervison are not just administrators, preachers, or counselors. They are theologians acting out the truths they confess. Students can put the experiences they have under supervision through the theological prism which will provide a depth to their thinking and their ministry.

Learning About Self

Students can usually learn about themselves from supervision better than any other way. The role of students in classroom courses is to learn about truths and the world and only about themselves from inference about how the students' racial, social, religious or psychological group fits into the generalizations presented in the classroom. Supervision gives the students specific data about who they are, how they function and how other people see them.

This can happen in supervision because the name of the game of supervision is "feedback." Again it is the analogy of holding mirrors up before the students so that they can see who they are in the perceptions of other people and in various situations. The feedback comes from their supervisors as they observe the student and evaluate the data over their experiences. The students also get feedback from their peers. This feedback is often more effective than from the supervisor because there is less likely to be a generation gap, they have a relationship with their peers in which information is already going back and forth between them and they know their peers are not the irrelevant "ivory tower" persons that they may expect the supervisor or professor to be. Students can also learn about themselves from laypeople. Laypeople know instinctively what they like about ministers and they can tell the students their impressions while other laypeople may be able to discern the reasons for their instincts and be able to give specifics when they give feedback to the students. The feedback from the laypeople is very important since in the end they are the ones to whom the ministry will be addressed and who must be satisfied with the students' ministry.

Many inventories have been developed to help students (and others) learn about themselves. These inventories cover intelligence, aptitude, psychological functioning, ways of relating, cognitive and affective approaches to life and personal strengths. The Minnesota Multiphasic Personality Inventory (M.M.P.I.) and the California Personality Inventory (C.P.I.) are instruments to give feedback about the psychological functioning and health of the person taking the inventory. They will also help the ministry students by pointing out issues which students need to be aware of such as defensiveness, the likelihood of their conforming to an institution, their introversion. The PF16 is an inventory which deals more with personal traits. While the PF16 is probably not as well validated as an inventory, many have found it helpful. It is less technical and difficult to interpret.

The FIRO-B is a simple inventory but gives an unusually accurate picture of a person's pattern of relating. It can be taken in a few minutes, scored immediately so that the interpretation can be immediate.

The Myers-Briggs Inventory seeks to measure the stance of a person and their reactions as to whether they will be intuitive, empirical feeling, etc. Knowing these things about oneself will help students to know why they react differently than many others do when they face a situation and also why they feel comfortable with other people who seem to react the way they do. It also gives them hints as to the most natural approach to learning which they have. The Theological Skills Index (T.S.I.) has been developed to help theological students understand what they mean by their "call" to ministry. It can be used by upper level students in colleges and is used by some theological seminaries as a part of the battery of tests and inventories taken upon admission.

J. W. Thomas, a consulting psychologist, developed the Bi-Polar Seminar with the assistance of personnel from the Perkins School of Theology at Southern Methodist University. This process determines the personal strengths of the students and helps them to see how a person with their strengths is likely to relate to people.

Sam Webb, of Georgia Institute of Technology, has developed a religious vocational aptitude inventory which can give the students feedback concerning the areas where they are more likely to feel comfortable in ministry. Some of the language in this inventory will have to be translated into the "in-house" language of each denominational group. There are inventories which will assist the students' self-knowledge about management styles, personnel relating and management philosophy.

Inventories give helpful feedback to ministry students and many people in supervision have found them to be worthwhile. However, there is nothing magical about inventories since they only measure the responses of the students and correlate them in more or less sophisticated ways with behavior patterns of other people. They are people who are test oriented so that they look for the majority of feedback to come out of inventories rather than experience. While supervision should take into account feedback from every possible source, the major focus of supervision is upon doing ministry and examining that ministry. Inventories which throw light upon that ministry and the patterns of the students' ministry will be helpful just as any insight into that ministry will be helpful. However, the role of supervision and the supervisor is not to be a psychotherapist but to be reflectors back to students what they see happening in their ministries.

During their supervised experience is a time for the students to learn about their depth of relationships. Some persons have a few relationships which are very deep and strong and others have many relationships but they are not nearly as intimate. Some students will find that they are able to establish relationships quickly, if not as deeply as others, but that others are able to establish relationships only guardedly. This is very important for students to know because their ministry will be made up of establishing relationships with people and they will be more comfortable as they know why they establish relationships the way they do.

One of the most important things which students can learn about themselves is "How do I come across?" Students (and others) often intend to come across one way but are perceived by others in another way. They may intend to be helpful but (in terms of T.A.) come across as critical parent. Students may attempt to be humble but it comes across as being either a false humility or "not okayness." Good intentions are not enough when we relate to other people because our good intentions are often subverted by habits, patterns or mannerisms. The period of supervision is a time for students to learn how they come across and students should insist that their supervisor, peers and laypersons give them clues about how they are coming across.

Students need to learn whether their basic stance is that of a doer or a thinker. Obviously every student will have skills in both doing and thinking but they will also have a natural stance in one or the other. Students need to know about their doing and thinking in order that they can utilize both and slow themselves down when they are about to face a thinking situation by doing or a doing situation by thinking. One of the best ways to get at this is by examining one's ministry log with the supervisor. The Bi-Polar Inventory is another way of learning this.

Is the student basically a minister or a layperson? Is the student more comfortable with other ministers or laypersons? This is information which ministry students need to have about themselves as they begin their ministry. There are students with a high ecclesiology who have a strong image of themselves as clergymen while other students are much more apt to see themselves on the same vocational status with all of the other persons in the church; they see themselves as lay people doing religious work full time. It is important for the students to know how they feel underneath about this issue because of the kinds of goal expectations that will be put upon them by a congregation which they will go to serve or the other ministry settings where they will serve. They will need to know the dangers of being so highly clergy-oriented that they have too great a gulf between them and the laypersons in the congregation and the danger of closing the space between themselves and laypersons who may have the need for those who minister to them to be more transcendent.

Students will be oriented either to persons or to programs. They will be able to give attention to people's needs and to program needs but they will operate out of one basic stance or the other. Students need to learn this about themselves because it will help them to develop sensitivities that they might not have naturally. Students who are more program-oriented will need to learn this about themselves in order to stop when they are about to launch one of the programs and ask what this will mean to persons who will be affected by the programs. On the other hand, students who are person-oriented need to examine what it means to be dealing so exclusively with persons as individuals that they do not develop the context in which the persons need to operate to be productive.

Students need to find out about their own reaction patterns to be on top of what is happening, rather than just reacting spontaneously to every situation. Students may need to change some reaction patterns and they will be able to do so when they learn what their reaction patterns are. More productive ways of reacting are just as legitimate. Students will only be able to learn their reaction patterns as they have experiences, react to them and have others help them to see patterns.

All people need stroking. Students need to become aware of their needs and how those needs are met. There are students who have an inordinate need for stroking and they need to get hold of the ego pattern before it becomes destructive. Other students will only be able to take negative stroking and they need to get in touch with what is going on with them and change their pattern. Students also give strokes or withhold strokes and they should become aware of their pattern of stroking other people.

Supervision will help students process the data which they get back in each of these areas. The students will probably not have an experience which will give them this data and the process to utilize this data outside of supervision. Learning about themselves is one of the most important things that students can do because they are young enough and malleable enough that they can change to be more what they want to be and what God has given them the gifts to be. During a student's lifetime, techniques and skills will change so that the skills they pick up now will become somewhat dated later in their ministry. Ideas will always be available but, again, the vocabulary and emphasis of ideas will change during the student's lifetime. The one thing that students cannot get away from is themselves so that it is much more important to learn about themselves than it is about either skills or ideas.

Deciding on a Ministry Vocation

Supervision is a time for students to try on ministry. Early Baptists in seventeenth century England would license a man to preach for a specific period of time (usually one year) in order for him to prove his gifts. After that initial period of time, if he had not had sufficient opportunity to prove his gifts, they would license him for another specific period of time. After the congregation was satisfied that the man had been called of God and had "proved his gifts," they would ordain him. This specific way of handling the trial period of ministry is largely gone now from Baptist life. However, supervision can be that time for "proving the gifts" of ministry students as they try on the ministry in a supervised ministry setting.

When supervision is used as a time for trying on ministry, it will be important for students to find out how comfortable they are with a ministry identity and ministry role. While it sounds heroic for students to commit themselves ultimately and irrevocably to the ministry before they have ever tried it out, it is far more realistic for them to "try out their calling and prove their gifts" and through that process come to determine whether or not the ministry has a divine calling for them. While students should not expect to become completely comfortable in the ministry identity and the ministry role in the supervision, they will be able to determine whether they *cannot* function in those roles. One of the most important ways for a student to use supervised ministry is to find out whether or not they should be in the ministry. Supervised ministry should be looked upon as a testing ground to determine the reality of one's call to ministry.

Supervised ministry will help not only with students' determination as to whether they should be in the ministry at all but also with the type of ministry they should be engaged in. There is a great variety of ministries available to students. There was a time in the church's history where most of the ministry had to do with preaching, teaching or being a missionary in a foreign land. Reflecting the complexity of modern society, the ministry has become very complex now. There are different ministry specializations including ministries in recreation, youth, age group specialties, social ministries, language ministries, denominational consultants, administration and many others. Supervised ministry should provide some opportunity for examining the multiplicity of ministry and giving students a view of the possibilities which they face. Beyond this, supervised ministry will offer the feedback to students so that they can know their strengths which they have to bring to ministry. They will be able to correlate those strengths with the strengths which will be needed in the various kinds of ministries which are available in the religious context. This feedback may come by way of inventories or feedback from peers, congregations and supervisors.

Examining the kind of ministry which students will want to pursue and the strengths they have and the strengths they need will give the students clues to the further education and training that they should pursue. They will be able to see whether they need a broad theological background, technical training built on that background, or whether they need specific technical training or whether just a broad theological background will be adequate. They will also be able to examine their training needs as far as lifelong learning is concerned and plan out what they will do at different steps in their ministry. The decision of a ministry vocation is dynamic. God is in constant conversation with us rather than having spoken once and never speaking again. This means that ministry students will need to recognize that the decisions which they make at the present time will need to be re-examined.

Developing Ministry Skills

Students need to learn what are the ministry skills. Students have entered schools to prepare for the ministry but all they have previously seen is the preacher in the pulpit or a youth worker organizing activities of a youth group, but are unaware of the organizational, counseling, administration and relational skills. One of the great advantages of supervision is that the students try out ministry and soon learn the kinds of skills that will be needed and whether those skills are consistent with their own strengths. In this day of specialization many young people going into the ministry want to specialize in a particular area without recognizing that they also need a wide range of ministry skills to fulfill the general functions of ministry so that they can perform the specialist functions of ministry. Regardless of the wide variety of ministry vocations, most ministries require a generalist.

The research skills that students develop in higher education are usually library research skills. These research skills are necessary for good academics and whether or not the students ever do original research which contributes to the body of the material of a discipline significantly, they learn about researching and they learn to appreciate the technique of researching. Ministers need researching skills, too, but usually a different kind of researching skill. Ministers usually need action research rather than library research. Action research is the kind which the minister will need to develop programs in a congregation or other ministry settings.

Students should find help in their own ministry skills by the modeling of ministry skills by their supervisors. While some of the modeling may come about unconsciously, supervisors should make a conscious effort to model skills for students. It is one of the most effective ways for the students to begin to get the feel about what it is to do the ministry that they have heard about. It is also a time in which the students can ask the supervisors about why they did certain things in the ministry.

During supervision, students will have the opportunity to practice skills in an environment which anticipates that the student will not be at a high proficiency level. They will be able to practice their skills without having the whole weight of mature responsibility upon them. With that kind of environment the practicing of skills should be less threatening to them and give them a feeling of freedom to experiment somewhat more. Students should not expect the proficiency which they hope to obtain later on. There is no reason to try to fake proficiency that is not there but on the other hand, students should not "bad mouth" themselves and what they are doing.

One of the advantages that students have under supervision is that they can get feedback about their skills and performance. Later on it will be extremely difficult to get competent feedback and usually feedback is either in the form of perfunctory compliments or extreme negativism in a crisis. Under supervision the students should get the feedback which is competent by a person who has been trained to give feedback. It is this way that the students can learn about their own skills and the skills which they need to develop. Students should not expect to end their supervised ministry with their skills perfectly honed. They should know what skills they are going to need by the time they finish and have made some progress toward developing those skills. But it will be necessary for them to continue developing those skills later in their ministry. A part of a good supervisory program for every student would be for them to develop a program for themselves of continuing training in the development of skills.

Student Goals and Learning Covenants

Students can use a covenant of learning advantageously for their supervision. The covenant of learning will set the goals for the students and also the limitations of expectations upon the students. By doing a covenant of learning, the students will sharpen their perspective on what is needed in the ministry and what they need to learn. There are two basic students' goals in a covenant of learning: learning and ministry. The students have a primary responsibility for learning because that is why the student is a student. However, students also have the responsibility for doing ministry because that is the only way they will really learn to do ministry. The parties who are involved in a covenant of learning include the student, the supervisor, the ministry setting and the director.

There are three different kinds of covenants: formal, informal and tacit. A formal covenant is one which is written out stating goals, responsibilities and accountabilities. An informal covenant is a contract between people although they cannot go to the extent of writing out what the conditions of the covenant will be. They have an understanding that each party in the covenant will carry out various responsibilities. We make these covenants every day of the week and usually every hour of the week. Such covenants may be as simple as saying to a friend, "I'll meet you downstairs for lunch at 12:15 p.m." A third type of covenant is a tacit covenant where one or more persons have a hidden agenda which they carry into the contracting without ever specifying these hidden terms of the contracting. They are left unspoken because one party usually does not want to admit a part of the covenant even though it is there. Usually both parties involved in the covenant understand the hidden innuendos even if they are not spelled out but trouble arises when one of the parties does not understand. Also difficulty arises when there is an attempt to change the tacit covenant because persons who can create tacit covenants may feel that they also have tacit permission to change the covenants. The covenant of learning of the students needs to be a formal covenant in order to cut down game playing and misunderstanding. Least of all, it should not be a tacit covenant where the students are playing the game, "I will write this out but you know that you won't hold me to it." Nor should it be a tacit covenant where the supervisors and the students have the tacit covenant "we will write this out for the director but we both know that we aren't going to pay any attention to it." The scope of a covenant of learning is limited and developmental. The covenant is limited by areas to be given attention, by time and level of expectation. It may not be possible to hit the right level of expectancies and limitations at first so the covenant may have to be adjusted through renegotiation.

Some assumptions will help facilitate good convenant processes. Clark Carney and S. Lynne McMahon listed some of these:

The Humility Assumption—I am not perfect, I would like to improve my interpersonal relationships and am willing to learn from you.
The Human Dignity Assumption—I value you and feel you are equal to me.
The Confidentiality Assumption—I will respect confidences which are entrusted to me.
The Responsibility Assumption—I will share equally with you in building and maintaining our partnership.
The Changeability Assumption—I can change and I am willing to try. Our relationship can change. We are not set in our ways.[7]

The process for building a covenant of learning will be determined a great deal by the format used by each institution. Generally, the school and the ministry setting both have some things which they will require in the covenant which will spell out the students' responsibility in relationship to those institutions. Once a student is selected or appointed to a ministry setting, the student must negotiate the areas in which he or she wants to grow and integrate that into the systems of the school and the ministry setting. Claus Rohlfs, Director of the Intern Program at Perkins School of Theology at Southern Methodist University in Dallas, has developed what he calls a SPIRO model to use to check the adequacy of covenants of learning. The word SPIRO is an acronym for "specificity, performance, involvement, realism and observability."[8] Specificity means that the covenant should be in concrete terms. Performance asks the question, "'What will the intern be doing?' Involvement deals with the extent of activity. Realism asks the question, 'Is it attainable within the time frame?' Observability means that the covenant should be stated in such a way that the intern and others can see the results and know when the goals have been reached.'"[9] The process of developing a covenant of learning must be built upon the realities of the ministry setting, the time frame, limitations of the supervisor and the students and upon the students' vision of what they need to achieve.

Schools often use two types of covenants: the check-off and the narrative. In the check-off covenant, the program lists skills or activities which students may wish to be involved in, students check the ones for which they will be responsible and the supervisor checks off the ones in which he will guide the students. This type of covenant has the advantages of making students aware of the many aspects of ministry and the many things for which they will be held accountable in ministry. It has the disadvantages of not being fully personal. Also students are not as likely to struggle with what it is they want to learn when all they have to do is check off a certain activity or skill rather than think through what they will achieve and how they will achieve it.

The narrative type of covenant is more sophisticated and is much more difficult to write up. The student must take the initiative to decide what it is that he or she needs to achieve in the ministry setting and how he or she will go about this. This forces the student to take some initiative which is not true with the check-off type of covenant. The students probably get a greater sense of ownership when they write up the narrative type of covenant but they are less likely to be thorough and see all the possibilities from the beginning. There may be some reason to combine a check-off and a narrative kind of covenant in order to take advantage of both types.

One difficulty with covenants is in determining when you have fulfilled the covenant. This evaluation sometimes is obvious and at other times is difficult to prove.

Areas in the ministry depend upon one spirit testing out another spirit so that there is no way to quantify those aspects. Well-written covenants will have within them how students will demonstrate that they have fulfilled each part of the covenant or who will evaluate to determine whether they have fulfilled each part of the covenant. The covenant of learning is the heart of the students' supervisory program since it lays out the ground rules by which the supervisors and the students will perform. The covenant of learning is the chain which links the school, the student, the supervisor, and the ministry setting.

The Students' Relationships

As I began developing a supervisory program at Midwestern Baptist Theological Seminary, I went to several denominational executives and asked them about the basic difficulties that ministers have so that we could develop ways to help students deal with those. The top item on the list of these denominational executives was relationships with people. While relationships are crucial for the minister, they also provide the major problem that most people have in the ministry. Students need to use supervision to become aware of the importance of relationships, how they relate to different people in different roles and how they relate in a variety of circumstances. Since it is easy to deceive ourselves about how we are coming across and relating, supervision is a good time for students to examine their relationships because they get feedback from enough sources to bring the perspective of reality to them. They are able to test out different ways of relating in order to get the feedback to find out whether the new relating patterns are more effective.

Students can begin examining relationships by examining their relationships with their supervisors. When they come to the end of their supervisory relationship, they can look back and develop a kind of taxonomy of relationship indicating what it was at the beginning, the end and the different places during the time that the relationship changed as well as what incidents brought about the change. Students should do the same thing with a variety of members of the congregation. They may be able to overlay the taxonomy that they have developed with the supervisor with a taxonomy with members of the congregation and see the difference in the way they relate to clergy and laypeople, to a supervisory of the students' program and those who have no such official relationship with the student. Students will want to look at their relationships with people in the community. They may need to ask the questions, "Why do I seek out members of the congregation and isolate myself from members of the community?" or "Why am I better received in the community than in the congregation?" or "Do I try to relate the same way and with the same intimacy with persons in the community as I do with members of the congregation?"

Students should look at how they relate to men and to women. Does the student get at the same depth of intimacy with both? Does the student move to intimacy with both at the same rate of speed? Do the students have trouble relating one sex or the other in official responsibilities? Are the students aware of the sexual overtones in their relationship with other persons?

While they are under supervision, students can profit from examining their relationships with their family in order to see if those relationships are healthy and whether they are likely to be able to stand the strains which ministry will place upon the family relationships. Supervisors may be able to help students who are willing to find vulnerable areas of relationships within the family such as time spent with the family, finances, mutuality, respect and common courtesies.

Supervision is a time to examine relationships with peers. A student's peers will be significant persons throughout ministry. Students will depend upon their peers for emotional strength during times of stress and for help during times of career transitions. Supervisors will want to help students see whether or not they are extractive in their relationship toward their peers, or whether they are reluctant to open up and let their peers know when they are vulnerable and need their support and help.

Students need to examine how they relate to different age groups. Students' relationships with youth often are on the basis of their being of like age rather than being ministers to the youth and at the same time they have difficulty relating to middle-aged people because the middle-aged people are reminders of their parents. They may relate to the elderly by allowing the elderly to make grandchildren out of them. There are occasions when young students have difficulty relating to those who are their own age and try to act in a manner that is more appropriate to maturity beyond their age without fully having that maturity. How students relate to different socio-economic groups is an important issue. This is also a dynamic aspect of students' relationships which should be looked at over a period of time to see how they change in the way they relate. Students who are involved in higher education move toward wanting to relate to higher socio-economic groups and develop less enthusiasm for ministering to those of lower socio-economic groups even if they came out of the lower socio-economic group. Some students develop a contempt of or a fear toward higher economic groups and are uncomfortable in the presence of members of the higher socio-economic group. Students may also develop a condescending attitude toward lower socio-economic groups. The products of the American system of higher education identify over-whelmingly with the middle and upper-middle socio-economic class creating difficulties for the educated ministry to identify and to minister to the poor and the wealthy. The supervisors and students should look at how the students relate to society figures. This will be a key to the students' developing programs, changing systems and ministering with a sense of comfort rather than a sense of intimidation.

The feedback which the students get from various sources can help them to find out about their pattern of relationships — whether they normally relate as the critical parent, the nurturing parent, adult, rebellious child or adaptive child. It is easy for students to develop a pattern of relating one way in all situations rather than being able to relate appropriately to each situation. Emotional and psychological maturity means that people have learned how to relate appropriately to different situations.

Students may feel comfortable relating to people in one position but uncomfortable in another. Therefore, students should use the feedback of supervision to find out how they react in over-under situations, formal-informal situations, structured and unstructured situations, intimate and surface relationships and how they are able to relate at different levels of relationships.

Students Supervised in Their Own Congregation

There are denominations, especially in the free church tradition, where many college and seminary students serve churches as pastors. The Home Mission Board of the Southern Baptist Convention has recognized that this is such a significant number among Southern Baptists that they have established an in-service guidance program to help student pastors believing that the student pastors who receive supervised field education help will be better pastors for the churches and, therefore, will help congregations be stronger.

A serious question must be raised about using an untrained student in the role of pastor while he or she is going to school. However, student pastors develop a learning readiness during the time that they are in school so that they can integrate academic material with the reality of the world more easily than those who do not have that exposure. Again, in spite of the advantages or disadvantages, the system is with us and may not change among many denominations. How, then, can we use student pastorates to be a good supervisory setting so that they can provide good learning experiences and not just work experiences?

The supervisor remains the key to the supervision experience of the students but the role is different where students are serving their own congregations. The supervisor does not know as much about the congregation, has no authority over the student with regard to the congregation and is not on hand to see the students perform their ministry with the congregation. The supervisor must make sure, especially in the free church tradition, that they do not interfere with the autonomy of the church where the student is the pastor. The supervisor can be a competent neighboring pastor, a denominational executive or a minister attached to a religious institution. The congregation has a role to play in the students' supervision because they are the ones who are on hand and receiving the ministry of the students. The congregation needs to be organized in such a way (such as lay committees) to give feedback to the students about what they actually observe and experience as a result of the students' ministry. The school also has a role because they become partners with the congregation in the teaching process. It is necessary for all parties to understand that the students who are pastors are responsible for all decisions and actions even though they are under supervision. The role of the supervisor is to give feedback and alternatives but it is the role of the students to be the pastors in the decision-making roles.

The ingredients of a supervised ministry program where the students are pastors are not substantially different from any other kind of a program except that a supervisor must be co-opted from another setting. There needs to be a supervisor, lay committee, routine supervision feedback, ministry experiences and evaluations. The students who are in pastoral roles face some specific problems. They have divided loyalties with the seminary, church and family. Often they do not receive an adequate salary. They may have no parsonage and, therefore, no place to stay while on the ministry field on weekends. Another disadvantage is that churches using students for pastors often develop a philosophy that the students will be there two or three years and will use them as stepping stones for another position and, therefore, they often do not take the student pastors seriously.

Learning to "Read" the Contexts of Ministry

One of the main things that students must learn to do is to "read" the contexts in which their ministries take place. An advantage of supervised ministry is that students can have someone looking over their shoulder while they learn to read contexts of ministry and give them clues about what is happening especially if they fall into gross error in their "reading." The temptation of every young minister is to try to deal with an individual or one situation without recognizing that there is a whole system involved and a whole society of persons involved instead of it being a simple situation. In dealing with a person or situation there is not just the one person or situation involved but the familiies, the whole congregation, the community and the denomination. Each of the contexts has complex interrelationships.

This means that students can use supervision to learn about formal and hidden agenda rather than entering their own ministry with a kind of naivete upon which they act that leaves them vulnerable. They can also learn about power; who has it, who wants it, what price the minister has to pay to get it, how long it usually takes for the power to shift and what are the legitimate and illegitimate uses of power. They will find out that the saying "blood is thicker than water" is very true especially in small communities where people are usually related. The members may criticize one another and they may even criticize their relatives but the pastors are outsiders regardless of whether they are right or not. When ministers criticize their congregations or members of the congregation, they will find that the community and the congregation will coalesce together and make the pastors the outsiders.

All of this means that supervision is a good place to learn about organizational development, grid systems for understanding organizations and critical paths of working with organizations. They may have found these subjects in their books on administration but they were more or less terms to be memorized rather than people named Joe, Bill, Mary, Betty.

In the same way students need to use supervision to

understand persons. They need to develop a kind of diagnostic process by which they are able to determine in a short period the relative healthfulness of the people with whom they are working. Students become quite skilled in reading books and being able to pick out the things that are important in the books which professors are likely to ask in class or on exams. These students also need to be able to learn to read contexts and find out what are the areas which will cause difficulty and what are the areas upon which they can depend upon to build their ministry.

Student Problems

Listing some of these student problems again may help to bring them into focus.

The students may have an unsatisfactory work level. They may be lazy, psychologically blocking or spread too thin.

There may be difficulty in the students' relationships with their supervisors. Supervisors may not be adequate or serious about their jobs. The informal relationship may be too much a father-son or a master-slave for there to be a good learning atmosphere. The students may be intimidated by the supervisor or by other persons in the ministry setting or even the setting itself.

Students may face a great deal of uncertainty in the supervisory process. Part of this may be uncertainty about expectations of them from the program, the supervisor and the ministry setting. They also may be uncertain about their ministry vocation. This may have to do with whether they ought to be in the ministry at all or whether they should be in a particular ministry specialty.

A general problem in the student internships is that the students either do not have enough significant work to do or they are given too much to do. Either way the students become frustrated by the internship and feel resentment. The resentment may be that they were not taken seriously enough as a mature young person or that they are being used by the supervisor or the setting.

A problem comes when there is either a change of supervisors or a change in the setting of supervision. Students develop covenants of learning with the original supervisors and settings and it short-circuits their program of learning if there is a change in either the supervisor or the setting. The students are likely to feel guilt or anger about the situation. If they were uncertain anyway about what was expected of them previously, now they are especially uncertain of what is expected of them either by the supervised program or by the setting.

Cultural differences between students and their supervisor or the settings bring serious problems. The problems become two way streets because the students are not understood when they function out of the context of their culture but students may also create problems by blaming any misunderstandings or failures in ministry upon the cultural differences and, therefore, play the "wooden leg" game. The differences are not just a matter of nationality but must also be thought of in terms of the sensitivity to the issue of women in ministry. There are instances where there is conflict between students and their mates about supervisory issues. Supervisors may press students about personal issues which involve behavioral patterns toward other people including their mates. The mates may feel that they are the ones who are also being supervised and rebel and resent the intrusion into an area. Supervision can also bring about some divided loyalties inasmuch as there is a claim on their time from the ministry setting as well as the school and the family. It may not just be the time it takes to do the ministry in the setting because the issues which are raised in supervision may cause a great deal of stress and the expenditure of psychic energy on the part of a student. This may cause other worker relationships to be affected by what goes on in supervision.

Whenever students who are receiving training in institutions of higher education move into a ministry setting, theological differences may surface. The students may be going through a period of theological transition which cannot be appreciated by people in the minstry setting.

A problem may be the students' commitment or at least the perception of the student's commitment on the part of the supervisor. Commitment may be spelled out in different ways among students now than it was during the period in which the supervisor was in school. However, the commitment may actually be less than is expected from one who is on the threshhold of becoming a minister.

Supervision may bring to the surface many other problems which are highly personal: hostility, immaturity, inexperience, shyness, verboseness, prejudice, defensiveness, compulsiveness, independence and unrealistic idealism.

FOOTNOTES
Chapter VI

[1]George I. Hunter Jr. and Ruth Deraney Khiralla, *Supervised Field Education Training Manual,* (Cambridge, Massachusetts: Episcopal Theological School, Rev. 1973), Part II, p. 20.

[2]Ibid.

[3]L. William Yolton and Ronald J. Gariboldi, "The Integration of Theology and Experience," *Fourteenth Biennial Consultation on Theological Field Education* (Berkeley, California: Graduate Theological Union, January 19-22, 1977), p. 106.

[4]James Whitehead and Evelyn Whitehead, "Report on Workshop E: Theological Reflection in Ministry," *Fourteenth Biennial Consultation on Theological Field Education* (Berkeley, California: Graduate Theological Union, January 19-22, 1977), p. 119.

[5]Francis O'Hare, unpublished paper presented at the B.T.I. Notre Dame Institute on Field Education, June, 1972.

[6]See *Theological Field Education: A Collection of Key Resources,* "Theological Reflection in Pastoral Theology," by James D. Whitehead, pp. 118-122, and "Theologizing in Field Education," by Carl B. Trutter, pp. 157-166, and the *Fourteenth Biennial Consultation on Theological Field Education,* "Report on Workshop E: Theological Reflection in Ministry," by James and Evelyn Whitehead.

[7]Clark Carney and S. Lynne McMahon, "The Interpersonal Contract," *The 1974 Annual Handbook for Group Facilitators,* ed. J. William Pfeiffer and John E. Jones, (LaJolla, California: University Associates Publishers, Inc., 1974), pp. 136-138.

[8]Claus H. Rohlfs, "The Covenant of Learning," *Fourteenth Biennial Consultation on Theological Field Education* (Berkeley, California: Graduate Theological Union, January 19-22, 1977), p. 73.

[9]Ibid.

Epilogue
The Ministry of Supervision

Supervision is a serious ministry—in fact it may be the most significant ministry that supervisors perform during their own ministry. They are molding the lives of the future representatives of the Kingdom of God. They are the human mothers and fathers of ministers. They are the ones who rock the spiritual cradle to shape the future world. Therefore, the ministry of supervision should be approached with seriousness, commitment, supervisory skills and prayer.

SELECTED BIBLIOGRAPHY

Books

American Association of Theological Schools. *Voyage, Vision, Venture,* Dayton, Ohio: American Association of Theological Schools, 1972.

Beisswenger, Donald F.; Hommes, Tjaard A.; and McCarty, Doran, ed. *Theological Field Education: A Collection of Key Resources,* Berkeley, California: Association for Theological Field Education, June, 1977.

Berne, Eric. *Games People Play,* New York: Grove Press, Inc., 1964.

Carney, Clark and McMahon, Lynne S. "The Interpersonal Contract," *The 1974 Annual Handbook for Group Facilitators,* ed. J. William Pfeiffer and John E. Jones, LaJolla, California: University Associates Publishers, Inc., 1974.

Ekstein, Rudolf and Wallerstein, Robert S. *Teaching and Learning of Psychotherapy,* New York: International Universities Press, Rev. 1972.

Feilding, Charles R. *Education for Ministry,* Dayton, Ohio: American Association of Theological Schools, 1966.

Feyereisen, Kathryn V.; Fiorino, A. John; and Nowak, Arlene T. *Supervision and Curriculum Renewal: A Systems Approach,* New York: Appleton-Century-Crofts, Educational Division, Meridith Corporation, 1970.

Glasse, James D. *Putting It Together In The Parish,* Nashville/New York: Abingdon Press, 1972.

Gleason, John J. Jr. *Growing Up To God,* Nashville/New York: Abingdon Press, 1975.

Hendrix, John and Householder, Lloyd, ed. *The Equipping of Disciples,* Nashville: Broadman Press, 1977.

Howe, Reuel. "Theological Education and Ordination," *Making the Ministry Relevant,* ed. Hans Hoffman, New York: Scribner and Sons, 1960.

Hunter, George I. Jr. and Khiralla, Ruth Deraney. *Supervised Field Education Training Manual,* Cambridge, Massachusetts: Episcopal Theological School, Rev. 1973.

Jongeward, Dorothy. *Everybody Wins,* Reading, Massachusetts: Addison-Wesley Publishing Co., 1973.

Keith-Lucas, Alan. *Giving and Taking Help,* Chapel Hill, North Carolina: The University of North Carolina Press, 1972.

Melnicoe, William B. and Mennig, Jan. *Elements of Police Supervision,* Beverly Hills, California: Glencoe Press, 1969.

Prestwood, Charles. *The New Breed of Clergy,* Grand Rapids, Michigan: William B. Eerdmans Publishing Company, 1972.

Readiness for Ministry report book. Vols. I and II, Vandalia, Ohio: Association of Theological Schools, 1975.

Rohlfs, Claus H. "The Covenant of Learning," *Fourteenth Biennial Consultation on Theological Field Education,* Berkeley, California: Graduate Theological Union, January 19-22, 1977.

Rouch, Mark. *Competent Ministry,* Nashville/New York: Abingdon Press, 1974.

Spicer, James. "The Place of Field Experience in Theological Education: Clues from Pastoral Theology," *The New Shape of Pastoral Theology,* ed. William B. Oglesby, Nashville: Abingdon Press, 1969.

Van Dersal, William R. *The Successful Supervisor in Government and Business,* New York, Evanston, San Francisco, London: Harper & Row Publishers, 1974.

Whitehead, James and Whitehead, Evelyn. "Report on Workshop E: Theological Reflection in Ministry," *Fourteenth Biennial Consultation on Theological Field Education,* Berkeley, California: Graduate Theological Union, January 19-22, 1977.

Wilson, J. Christy, ed. *Ministers in Training,* Princeton, New Jersey: The Directors of Field Work in the Theological Seminaries of the Presbyterian Church, USA, 1957.

Yolton, L. William and Gariboldi, Ronald J. "The Integration of Theology and Experience," *Fourteenth Biennial Consultation on Theological Field Education,* Berkeley, California: Graduate Theological Union, January 19-22, 1977.

Journals and Magazines

Bergland, James W. "Field Education as Locus for Theological Reflection," Theological Education, Vol. V, No. 4 (Summer, 1969).

Journal of the Academy of Parish Clergy, (April, 1971), pp. 63-64.

Journal of the Academy of Parish Clergy, (March, 1975), pp. 43-44.

Kadushin, Alfred. "Supervisor-Supervisee: A Survey," *Journal of Social Work,* May, 1974.

Kadushin, Alfred. "Games People Play in Supervision," *Journal of Social Work,* July, 1968.

Klink, Thomas W. "Supervision As a Routine Process in Professional Education for Ministry," *Duke Divinity Review,* 1968.

Lehner, George F.J. "Team Development Trainer's Workshop," *Public Administration Review,* March / April, 1974.

Lloyd, Barton M. "Key Issues in the Personal Preparation of Clergy," *Theological Education,* Summer, 1969, Supplement 1.

McCarty, Doran C. "Supervising Minister of Music Students," *The Southern Baptist Church Music Conference Journal,* 1978.

Myers, William C. "Process in a First-Year Pastoral Training Program," *Theological Education,* Summer, 1969, Supplement 1.

Southard, Samuel. "Criteria for Evaluating Supervisors-in-Training," *The Journal of Pastoral Care,* Vol. XVII, Winter, 1963.

Steere, David A. "An Experiment in Supervisory Training," *The Journal of Pastoral Care,* Vol. XXIII, No. 2, December, 1969.

Wheelis, Allen. "How People Change," *Commentary,* May, 1969.

Zimmerman, Jervis S. "The View from the Field: A Supervising Pastor's Experience in the In-Parish Pastoral Studies Program," *Theological Education,* Vol. III, No. 3, Spring, 1967.

Unpublished Material

Cutrer, Clyde. "Contract for Learning—Youth Music."

Matarazzo, Ruth G. "Factors Relevant to Teaching Psychotherapy and Evaluating Trainee Performance," University of Oregon Medical School.

O'Hare, Francis. Paper presented at the B.T.I. Notre Dame Institute on Field Education, June, 1972.

Southard, Samuel. "The Process of Student Supervision," Georgia Mental Health Institute, Atlanta, Georgia, 1971.